Ausiàs March
Verse translations of thirty poems

Ausiàs March
Verse translations
of thirty poems

Introduction, text, translation and notes by
Robert Archer

BARCINO·TAMESIS
BARCELONA/WOODBRIDGE 2006

In memory of my mother & father
Daphne Joan Archer & Edwin Leonard Archer

First published 2006
by Tamesis
in association with Editorial Barcino

ISBN 1 85566 130 6
COPYRIGHT DEPOSIT: B-21.647-06

Tamesis is an imprint of Boydell & Brewer Ltd
PO Box 9, Woodbridge, Suffolk IP12 3DF, UK
and of Boydell & Brewer Inc.
668 Mt Hope Avenue, Rochester, NY 14620, USA
www.boydellandbrewer.com

Editorial Barcino, S. A.
Montseny 9. 08012 Barcelona, Spain
www.editorialbarcino.com

Designed and typeset by Jordi Casas

Printed in Spain by
Grup 3

Cover illustration:
*Jaume Cabrera. The Three Marys, Nicodemus and angels.
Detail from a painting on wood from Torroella de Montgrí.
First third of fifteenth century (Museu d'Art de Girona).*

Contents

POEMS OF PRAISE AND BLAME

Preface

To CLAIM, AS MANY HAVE, that Ausiàs March is the greatest poet in fifteenth-century Europe, is an embarrassment in two ways. Firstly, because there are no real objective criteria for such a claim. In what sense and for what is he the greatest, and how is it possible for all but the most wide-ranging expert to verify this assertion? Secondly, the label of 'the greatest poet in fifteenth-century Europe' seems for those who know his poems to be far too restrictive. March did indeed write in the first half of the fifteenth century, but much of his work transcends the boundaries of his historical epoch and the literary context in which he wrote. A good part of it lives as poetry as much today as when he wrote. This is the even grander claim that needs to be made on his behalf, although this one is easily verified: 'Llija mos dits' –'Read my poems'– as March himself said. This anthology of verse translations is an attempt to allow those who read poetry, but are not necessarily fluent in medieval Catalan, to take up March's invitation.

The translations are based on versions in prose on which I had worked over a period of many years and which were intended essentially as an aid to March's original text. While in the early stages of preparing this volume, with prose versions in mind, I suddenly realised an all too obvious truth: that for the reader of poetry, exegetic prose translations can tell us much about what is in the poetry, but can give little sense of the poetry itself. For the purposes of poetry only a verse translation will do. José María Micó's excellent Spanish versions of 2004 pointed the way.[1] It was a matter of

---

[1] Costanzo Di Girolamo & José María Micó, ed. and trans., *Ausiàs March. Páginas del cancionero* (Madrid- Buenos Aires-Valencia: Editorial Pre-Textos, 2004).

plucking up the temerity to produce another version, this time in verse. The thirty poems in this volume show that temerity at least has not failed me. There was only one possible metre for translating March: the iambic pentameter. Rhyme, of course, obligatory for most of the genres in which March wrote his decasyllabic stanzas, has not been a requirement for the English pentameter since at least as early as Shakespeare; moreover, March himself, like Shakespeare, for his more meditative verse, sometimes had recourse to unrhymed stanzas. There was, besides, an attendant danger, namely that the need to rhyme would inevitably create distortions in meaning, totally avoidable ones for which the effect of rhyme cannot compensate.

The text of March's poems used here is that of my critical edition.[2] I have introduced several changes of punctuation, and have corrected some printing errors. The Roman numbers of the poems correspond to the order established by Amédée Pagès in his critical edition of 1912-1914.[3]

The verse translations were all produced between February and September 2005, a short space of time for such an enterprise, and I am very grateful to Stephen Boyd and Dominic Keown who sent me rapid and valuable responses to some of the early drafts, but am especially indebted to Gareth Walters who read all the poems in his capacity as the publisher's reader and made many valuable suggestions, all of which (including one or two complete lines) I have incorporated into the final version.

Many of the prose versions that underlie these translations benefited from the criticism, detailed and characteristically kindly, of Arthur Terry. His posthumous verse translation of Gabriel Ferrater's *Les dones i els dies* – in my opinion, his finest work as a translator – has encouraged me to believe that Catalan poetry can indeed live in English.[4]

R.A., Dobřichovice, Czech Republic, December 2005

---

[2] Robert Archer, ed., *Ausiàs March. Obra completa* and *Ausiàs March. Obra completa: Apèndix* (Barcelona: Barcanova, 1997).

[3] Amadeu Pagès, ed., *Les obres d'Auzias March*, 2 vols. (Barcelona: Institut d'Estudis Catalans, 1912-1914).

[4] Arthur Terry, trans., 2005. *Gabriel Ferrater. Women and Days*, with Introduction by Seamus Heaney (Todmorden: Arc).

Introduction

To Ausiàs March are attributed 128 poems, totalling some 10,000 lines, produced in the course of thirty years or so in the midst of what seems to have been a demanding period spent consolidating the family fortune and its social position and adapting to the realities of the increasingly mercantile context of life in and around his native Valencia. His work, all in Valencian Catalan, survives in thirteen manuscripts, the earliest of which date back to the second half of the fifteenth century (as well as five editions from the mid sixteenth century). This is a prodigious number of copies for a poet from his period, and the wide variety of the poems included in them (no single source contains all his work) and the range of variant readings between them suggest that there were many more manuscripts than the ones known today. March was thus both hugely productive and widely known during his life and for some time afterwards. That he is not exactly a household name in the hispanic cultural world and beyond is largely due to history and politics: with the fall of the Islamic kingdom of Granada and the discovery of the New World in 1492, Spanish was able not only to confirm its major status in the Peninsula, but also to establish itself in a continent where the demographic developments of the ensuing five centuries would turn it into one of the world's most powerful languages. In the meantime, Catalan remained within its fifteenth-century boundaries and suffered the inevitable external assault and internal assimilation of the neighbouring world language.

At the time March wrote his poems he would have felt that he was using one of the major languages in the world as it was then known. It was one of the official languages of the Crown of Aragon under which the Kingdom of Valencia fell, in spite of the recent occupation of the throne by a member of the Castilian-speaking Trastamaran dynasty (Alfonso 'the Magnanimous'), and the Crown of Aragon was the major player in the Christian Mediterranean. It was the language of the important city where he was born and which he lived in or near all his life, the language of his own class (the knights) and of the other Christian classes of Valencia. The influence of Castile as a linguistic power still essentially did not extend beyond its peninsular boundaries.

And yet March's use of Catalan is more surprising than it might first appear, since all his predecessors in the poetic tradition in which he wrote used a linguistic mish-mash of Catalan and Provençal, which was deemed essential both for the transmission of concepts inherent to the tradition, and because of the need to find rhymes (the Provençal-Catalan tradition had an arsenal of these, neatly catalogued by one of March's uncles). March took the decisive step into a language which was recognisably Catalan, and, more specifically, Valencian Catalan. It is a rather bitter irony that nearly six hundred years later, with 350 million or so speakers of Spanish and, at best, some ten million using the various forms of Catalan, his work now belongs to a literature labelled as that of a 'minority' language in relative demographic terms. Doubly ironic, since he almost certainly never had as many readers in his lifetime, or during the vogue his work enjoyed in the mid sixteenth century, as he has now. But by then –the ironies multiply– the poetic language he had forged had become largely unrecognisable to Valencians themselves as essentially the same one as they spoke in the street (commentators of the time referred to his poetic language as 'lemosín', assuming that it was some form of Provençal). All these factors have conspired, and conspire still, in spite of the revival of interest in March since he was championed by Romantic critics in the mid nineteenth century, to turn his work into, at best, a still relatively unfrequented corner of studies on the literature of Spain and the Middle Ages.

The claim is made here that March's work continues to be something to which we can relate as living poetry rather than as merely an object of philological interest, and we can explore the reasons why this might be so a little later. But we first need to ask what March was trying to do, in the context in which he lived, when he wrote all this verse. The court was situated across the Mediterranean in Naples, for much of March's productive life; Alfonso left the Peninsula in 1432, never to return. March certainly had many dealings with Alfonso's abandoned Queen at various points in his

life, and there are also two versions of a poem addressed to Alfonso, asking
for the gift of a falcon (March had been his head falconer for some years),
as well as a poem written for the influential court figure of Antoni Tallan-
der, but there is no evidence he was in Naples himself or that, if he had
been, he had had there a role of any importance. March, like other literary figures in Valencia, writes, if not quite on the margins of Empire, then
not from its cultural centre either. Besides which, the king's taste was for
verse that lent itself for performance, with or without music, the kind that
would help produce a brilliant courtly milieu along Italian Renaissance
lines. But March's peculiar mode of writing could have little place
in Alfonso's court (it is not known if any of his poems were meant for
performance). Clearly, though, he had in Valencia an appreciative
audience: he addresses his readers at several points, and he refers at one
point to not being understood by some. No one can write as much as he
did in that period without an audience; the Romantic concept of the
lonely artist who writes for himself has no place in fifteenth-century
Valencia. By the 1440s he is clearly recognized as a major poet. The Mar-
qués de Santillana, a poet of considerable talent himself, refers to him in a
famous account of contemporary poetry in the Peninsula, as 'a great poet'
('gran trovador'), and March is also one of a number of troubadours and
later poets whose work is quoted in a long misogynous piece by Francesc
Ferrer, written between 1448 and 1449 (he quotes from March's poem
XLII, an attack on a lady and her merchant lover).[5]

In much the same way as his predecessors, March's guiding objective
poetically was to write what the literary theorists of the old school called the
novell dictat or 'new poem' –one which was recognizably part of the tradition that all readers knew, and yet was fresh and different. In a way that the
theorists of his uncle's generation would not have approved, there is
already a fundamental freshness in the use of a language that no longer
relied, except very sporadically, on the poetic *koiné*. It is reasonable to
assume that his early efforts in verse would have been written in Provençal-
Catalan like those of his brilliant contemporary Jordi de Sant Jordi (along-
side whom he fought for Alfonso), but if they were, nothing has survived.
The important thing is that, from the start, March's extant work lurches off
the dwindling path of Provençal-Catalan and onto a new road of its own
construction, using it to work out fresh ways of developing the traditional.

    [5] Francisco López Estrada, ed., *Las poéticas castellanas de la Edad Media* (Madrid:
Taurus, 1984), p. 58; *Francesc Ferrer. Obra completa*, ed. Jaume Auferil (Barcelona:
Barcino, 1989), pp. 93, 231-232.

Whether March also had a conscious political motive for moving over almost completely to Catalan, we can only guess. Certainly the resurgence of Castilian (but also of Italian) in the Neapolitan court may have made the use of the old Provençal-Catalan idiolect seem redundant in a way it had not been until the crown passed to the Trastámaras; he may have felt isolated enough from where he wrote in Valencia without the linguistic isolation that writing in the old poetic language would possibly have meant, and to continue to use it may also have seemed politically imprudent. Catalan was at least an official language. Then, too, the inroads that Italian had made as a literary language, in masterpieces that were increasingly well known from the end of the fourteenth century onwards, already pointed to the legitimacy of using the spoken language as a basis for literary production.[6]

Other major differences introduced by March into the practice of poetry are ones of thematic perspective. In particular, in what we can term the 'love poetry', which makes up the bulk of his work, the emphasis shifts, much further than the tradition had usually allowed, away from discussion of unrequited passion and towards an introspective analysis of the kind of love the poet feels: physical, physical-spiritual, or spiritual. All this is worked out with reference to Scholastic psychology, sometimes in a fragmented way, but occasionally in a much more discursive form (for instance, in much of the long poem XCII). The lady in the love poems functions as the sign for 'woman', with all the misogynous medieval charge that this carries (see poem XLII), and is the source of a closely analysed perplexity. No *donne angelicate* here; March's one poem of praise for a woman (XXIII) –surely one of the great poems of its kind– lauds the fact that the lady is not a virgin, but rather the mother of noble progeny, beautiful in form but with an even more beautiful brain.

In all his poems March strove to achieve novel variations on the conventions of the tradition by using the full gamut of devices which its poets had employed for centuries and which its theorists had formulated in their rhetorical manuals. A careful reading of all March's poems reveals that no two are alike: each answers in its own way the need to produce something different within the still fairly tight boundaries of convention. March particularly favoured the use of the extended simile. His work abounds in simile images (nearly all of which are applied to the poet him-

---

[6] Di Girolamo & Micó, pp. 15-16.

self) that are drawn from the realities of medieval life, though often through the mediation of literature (the physician and his patient, the ship at sea, the page at court, a mother and her child, the hermit) or from bestiaries or the Bible (the turtle-dove, apocryphal accounts of St Paul, or even Christ); he strings them together and constructs almost entire poems from them (see poems I and II, for instance), and in one piece (LXVIII) he attempts a prolonged negative simile followed by a positive one ('I am not like A, but am like B').[7] Another frequent rhetorical device is the extended allegory which includes the use of personifications (a good example is poem XI). Hyperbole abounds, but is transmuted into many forms: take, for instance, poem XLVI where the return to the addressed lady is transformed into a projected voyage of apocalyptic dimensions, or the whole discourse on 'sadness' as a way of life in poem XXXIX. A more spectacular innovation is seen in poem XXXII: a poem on a purely moral-philosophical theme, which develops Aristotelian ideas on the good, ends disconcertingly with a traditional address to a lady in which the poet pleads for her mercy; the reader is left to make sense of the juxtaposition of two apparently disparate discourses. But many of March's developments of the *novell dictat* can only be appreciated in the context of his output as a whole, and these take far more subtle forms than the bold rhetorical devices mentioned. It is in this area that the aesthetic gap between March's contemporary readers and ourselves begins to yawn wider.

And yet it was the same impetus to forge something new with each fresh *dictat* that led to the creation of poems that are almost immediately accessible to us. These poems constitute, in effect, new genres, in so far as they are without clear generic antecedents. Half the space in this selection is given over to these poems, precisely because they are so original, as well as so powerful. Six of them (XCII-XCVII, known since the sixteenth century as the *cants de mort*) concern grief over the death of a woman who is clearly identified as the poet's wife: she is referred to in the first of them (XCII, 180) as his 'wife-beloved' (*muller aimia*), a striking composite phrase combining the term for a spouse and the traditional Provençal word for the beloved lady addressed in love poems, while the final lines of the same composition refer to the reunion on Judgement Day of poet and woman as 'one flesh', a concept of biblical origin fundamental to the sacrament of mar-

[7] For a study of March's use of comparisons, see Robert Archer, *The Pervasive Image. The Role of Analogy in the Poetry of Ausiàs March*, Purdue University Monographs in Romance Languages, no. 17 (Amsterdam: John Benjamins, 1985).

riage.[8] A poet in the tradition in which March was nurtured was generically restricted for an occasion of this kind to the *planh* (the Latin *planctus*), a composition in which there would be praise for the deceased, and an invitation to join the poet in his grief. There is none of this in March's six poems: no praise of any kind. In the Italian tradition, which March also knew, there was also the model of Petrarch's sonnets, *In morte di madonna Laura*; here March differs even more, since, very far from assuming that the lady has gone to Heaven, he expresses the fear at several points that she is in purgatory or worse. The nature of the fear itself is unconventional; March dreads her damnation since, as he sees it, it necessarily implies his own; indeed, in one poem, he expresses his belief that he could be held responsible for the sins that have damned her.

The concern with the impact of events on himself is a continuation into this context of what can be found in most of his love poems. But in the six poems on grief this I-centredness takes two further forms. In the first place, the lady's death opens up an avenue that for the poet of the love poems had always seemed inaccessible: that of loving with the spirit alone, at last freed of the body. Many lines are devoted to analysing the new possibilities of spiritual love; in the first poem (XCII) in particular March constructs a theory of love justifying his belief in these possibilities. The second form of introspective discourse concerns the experience of bereavement itself. March, well aware of the Stoico-Christian proscription of prolonged mourning for the dead, nevertheless presents a fragmentary study of grief. There are striking parallels with the experience that C. S. Lewis describes in his own account of personal loss in *A Grief Observed*: the sense of absence and longing, the way in which objects and times of the day bring the loved one to mind, the feeling of guilt experienced by the bereaved.[9]

Misgivings about the fate of his soul are central to the other generically original poem included in this volume (poem CV, known, also since the sixteenth century, as the *cant espiritual*). Here in twenty-eight stanzas of

[8] The order of the *cants de mort* in the most reliable sources is actually XCII-XCV, XCVII, XCVI, but here we follow tradition in keeping the order established by Amédée Pagès in his critical edition of 1912-1914. The wife to which the poems refer is almost certainly Joana Escorna, to whom March was married from 1443 until her death in 1453 or 1454, although the evidence is purely circumstantial; but the theory cannot be discounted that the reference is to his first wife, Isabel Martorell (she died in 1439 after less than a year of marriage); or, indeed, it may be that some of the the six poems refer to one wife and some to the other, and that their collection together in the manuscript sources and early editions is for reasons of obvious thematic similarity rather than chronology.

[9] Originally published in 1961 under the pseudonym of N. W. Clerk and republished under his own name in 1964 (London: Faber).

unrhymed verse March achieves and maintains an emotional pitch quite unmatched by anything in the Iberian Peninsula before the second half of the sixteenth century. The poem, essentially a prayer, addressed entirely to God, swings dramatically between the extremes of despair and hope as March considers the implications of the doctrines of predestination, free will, grace, divine will, and omniscience that had concerned not only late fourteenth- and early fifteenth-century preachers in the Crown of Aragon like Francesc Eiximenis and St Vincent Ferrer, but also a number of Castilian poets in the early fifteenth century.[10] March depicts himself wrestling with the tangle of ideas which writers of theological treatises on the subject themselves saw as ultimately unresolvable by man (ideas which still raise difficulties for twenty-first-century thinking Christians). If God is omniscient, then he must know the destiny of each man's soul; if he knows, from his eternal present, that some are destined to be damned, why did He create them in the first place and then allow them to use their free will to commit the sins which would justify their damnation? March clearly struggles to accept the Church's position, which was that God never wills the damnation of any soul, but passively permits some to condemn themselves, while actively extending grace to others. The poem is exceptional in many ways, not least the frankness with which March confronts head-on his lack of love for God, and in the end does not hold out much hope that he will attain this virtue of charity necessary for salvation. Striking too is its dramatic form: March does not write a poetic report of his struggle, but seems rather to act out as immediate event the twists and turns of a mental process, frequently lurching suddenly to a different viewpoint, while offering no explanation of why the change has taken place.

It is not difficult for a twenty-first-century reader to relate to so powerful a poem on the question of the afterlife, nor to those on grief: human emotions and anxieties still bridge miraculously the chronological gap between a fifteenth-century Valencian knight and ourselves. But what of the other pieces? Why and how, as is claimed here, do some of them still live as poetry, arising as they do from long-abandoned formulations of literary love relationships that can have little bearing on the way we live our lives or even the way we love?

We might attempt the beginnings of an answer by focusing on March's use of two rhetorical devices –conceit and metaphor– in poem XXVIII.

---

[10] For a discussion of this, see Robert Archer, 'Ausiàs March and the *Baena* Debate on Predestination', *Medium Aevum*, 62 (1993), 35-50.

This starts with a passage of description of the external world that is most untypical of March (he normally refers to the world outside the poetic 'I' through the medium of the extended simile); only after this descriptive passage does he introduce the figure of the poet, at which point the poem turns inwards:

XXVIII

Lo jorn ha por de perdre sa claror
quan ve la nit que espandeix ses tenebres.
Pocs animals no cloen les palpebres
4   e los malalts creixen de llur dolor;
los malfactors volgren tot l'any duràs
perquè llurs mals haguessen cobriment;
mas jo, qui visc menys de par en turment
8   e sens mal fer, volgra que tost passàs.

E d'altra part faç pus que si matàs
mil hòmens justs menys d'alguna mercé,
car tots mos ginys jo solt per trair-me.
12   E no cuideu que·l jorn me n'excusàs,
ans, en la nit treball rompent ma pensa
perquè en lo jorn lo traïment cometa.
Por de morir o de fer vida estreta
16   no·m tol esforç per donar-me ofensa.

Tornada

Plena de seny, mon enteniment pensa
com aptament lo llaç d'amor se meta.
Sens aturar, pas tenint via dreta.
20   Vaig a la fi si mercé no·m defensa.

Day sees with terror how its last light fades
and night comes, spreading darkness in its path.
Wide-eyed, small creatures dare not welcome sleep;
4   *the sick and weak endure redoubled pain.*

Now evil men come out to do their worst:
cloaked by the dark, they'd have it last all year.
Not I: of me need none fear harm, tormented
8 *like no other: I long for night to pass.*

And yet, if I had murdered a thousand
guiltless men I could do no worse: each night
I set my wits to plot my betrayal.
12 *And don't suppose the dawn will bring respite:*
all night I'm busy wrenching from my mind
how best to shape the next day's perfidy.
What fear holds death or else the prison cell
16 *in one who's traitor to his very self?*

Envoi

Beauteous Wisdom, there's none to blame but me
if Love has placed his noose around my neck.
The road runs straight, and I don't drag my steps.
20 *The end's in sight: will pity send reprieve?*

The dynamics of the poem hinge on the rhetorical device of the 'conceit' in which the poet shows how two apparently irreconcilable terms are linked in a way we had not perceived previously, but which is now revealed to us as their irreconcilability is worked out and resolved in the second stanza. The whole point of the poem lies in this revelation. What March seems to be saying on the surface of things could be formulated as a trite paradox: 'the meek do the most harm', a counter-rational statement of the kind 'A is X'. But what gives these lines their power is that this counter-rational statement is then resolved through the explanation of line 11 ('I set my wits to plot my betrayal') and through the subsequent expansion in the rest of the second stanza of this line's untranslatable punning metaphor *soltar ginys* ('to set the traps' / 'use all my wits'). Here the conceit has a heuristic function: we are not merely *told* this important truth; we are led to it through a *process* of revelation. This poem, even though it is constructed with the conventions of the courtly love lyric, operates as much more than a statement about the sufferings of unrequited love. The poem turns out to be a metaphoric description of the self-destructive urges that afflict all but the most blessed personalities. In this, of course, the meaning of the poem moves on a level that lies above (or below) its literary context. Part of its power lies in the way the revelation is made through the rhetorical device of the conceit, drawing on a series of metaphors that make immediate the inherent truth of the situation without having to call up any of the jaded aphorisms such as 'man is his own worst enemy' with which the same truth is often observed (and immediately forgotten).

Metaphor is the other aspect of this poem that needs to be discussed. It is a rhetorical device that permeates March's work in an obvious way, one of the many to which he had recourse in his efforts to produce more and still more *novells dictats*. But for a certain school of modern thought (the cognitivist approach to metaphor), metaphor underlies not only poetry, but also much of the way we think about the world and conceptualize it. Many of those metaphors, only half-glimpsed by us most of the time, coincide with many of the ones that are explicitly used by March.

The basic theory, developed by George Lakoff and collaborators, posits the essential metaphoricity of much of the way we perceive our own world and our existence in it.[11] This arguably does not extend as far as the theory claims, as several critical voices have pointed out, but it does expose the extent to which our cognition of the world, the way we perceive it and understand it, relies on a number of basic and irreplaceable conceptual metaphors such as LIFE IS A JOURNEY, LOVE IS A JOURNEY, or IDEAS ARE FOOD; from these conceptual metaphors metaphorical linguistic expressions are derived such as 'keep right on to the end of the road', 'the long and winding road that leads to your door', or a statement like 'all his book has in it are raw facts, half-baked ideas and diluted theories.' Lakoff and collaborators identified scores of such conceptual metaphors underlying metaphorical linguistic expressions or even concepts which we would not normally think of as metaphors at all (and here they may simply be mistaken). But it is precisely the existence of such conceptual metaphors across time, and the need of human beings to revert to them by means of countless metaphorical linguistic expressions, that perhaps begins to explain the role of metaphor in earlier literature as the means by which we can access a poetic 'world' even where all the other referents may seem alienating.

That is, the immediacy of meaning in March's poem XXIII is possible because we continue to share with March and his readers these same basic

---

[11] George Lakoff & Mark Johnson, *Metaphors We Live By* (Chicago: University of Chicago Press, 1980), and especially George Lakoff & Mark Turner, *More Than Cool Reason. A Field Guide to Poetic Metaphor* (Chicago: University of Chicago Press, 1989). See also Zoltán Kövecses, *Metaphor. A Practical Introduction* (Oxford: Oxford University Press, 2002) and the salutary criticisms of Lakoff & Turner in the review by Ray Jackendoff & David Aaaron, *Language*, 67 (1991), 320-338.

metaphors, and continue to use them to construe the world –conceptual metaphors which can be expressed in the sloganized small– capitals form that cognitivists work with such as LIFE IS LIGHT, LIFE OF HUMAN BEINGS IS A DAY, SIGNIFICANT IS BIG (INSIGNIFICANCE IS SMALL), CHEERFUL IS SUNNY, BAD IS BLACK, CHANGE OF STATE IS CHANGE OF LOCATION, DEATH IS NIGHT, EVENTS ARE ACTIONS, THE MIND IS A CONTAINER, PURPOSES ARE DESTINA-TIONS, DEATH IS GOING TO A FINAL DESTINATION, etc. It could be argued that all these conceptual metaphors –the basis of countless linguistic metaphorical expressions, including poetic ones– bear upon the process by which we are able to relate to what March is saying in this poem.

This perception of metaphor as something 'we live by', to use the title of one of Lakoff's books, at the root of the way we construe the world, just might help explain the anomaly of our readerly habitation of poetic worlds constructed with the literary language of the fifteenth century. There seems to be a considerable area of overlap between what is in the text and what we as later readers bring to it. This in itself suggests a mode of perceiv-ing the world and of referring to it that is at least partly shared by poets like March and those who read their work today. Readerly competence has to be assumed of course: we need to know sufficient about the context of the poem to be able to avoid making grossly false assumptions and, thanks to such knowledge, we are able to jettison irrelevant parts of our own concep-tual and cultural baggage. But such readerly competence –essentially, intellectual knowledge– does not explain how we are able to relate on an extra-intellectual level to a poem written in a period far distant from our own. Why is there a sense of recognizable experience in the reading of such poems? Because of the shared experiential basis of some kinds of concep-tual metaphor, the Lakoffians would say. This has surely to be one of the reasons why some of this poetry can actually mean something to us –indeed, mean a great deal– at an affective level, and do so at such a huge temporal and cultural remove.

But each reader will also find his or her own reasons for relating to March's poems and, in a curious way, the gap between text and reader that language and history create only serves (as it does with Shakespeare) to augment the sense of vital immediacy and conceptual power. The transla-tions in this volume are written in the belief that, even in the literary lan-guage of twenty-first-century England, something of this immediacy and power will manage to make itself felt.

Biographical note

AUSIÀS MARCH WAS BORN in 1400 in Valencia, and lived most of his life in the town of Gandia on the coastal plain of Valencia, and also perhaps in the nearby village of Beniarjó. The Marchs had been connected with the region since the final Christian reconquest in the mid fifteenth century, but it is not until the 1330s that March's grandfather establishes his branch of the family, which had its roots in Barcelona, in Valencia. His father, Pere, was a top-ranking court administrator, closely connected to the king, and it was through him that the family acquired its noble status in 1360. March was thus born as a second generation knight. As early as 1415, before he was knighted (this happened some time in or after 1419), Ausiàs is mentioned as a representative of his class at the royal court in Valencia that year.

In late youth and early manhood, March distinguished himself in Alfonso's first military campaigns in Sardinia and Corsica in 1420, and at the end of 1424 he was with the army that was sent to deal with pirates operating off the coast of North Africa and Sicily, and was present during the attack on the island of Djerba. In 1420 he is mentioned for the first time in relation to Queen Maria (subsequently regent during Alfonso's long absence), and in 1425, in consideration of his military service, the king confirms the rights and privileges in Beniarjó and other villages that had been conferred on his father a few decades before. But he does not join Alfonso in the later expedition to Italy. Instead, as far as is known, he remained in Valencia, administering his lands and attending to family business. However, in both 1427 and 1428 he is mentioned with the title of 'head falconer' of the king, and again in 1434 and 1444 (but without the title) he is described as breeding and caring for royal falcons. One of his poems, certainly written after 1447, as it alludes very clearly to Lucrezia d'Alagno who is linked openly with the king from this time, is a request for a falcon with which to hunt and thus keep himself from mischief in his old age (the request is especially ironic since the king writes to March in 1446 asking him to send to Naples one of Ausiàs's own falcons). Such activities would have meant that for the earlier years at least March would have spent some time in the Albufera, the area surrounding the lagoon near Valencia, engaged in hunting and in rearing the birds.

But aside from this, March's life in Valencia and Gandia seems largely to have involved the zealous protection and exercise of the seigneurial privileges of the Marchs. Some of these privileges he saw diminished in favour of his immediate overlords (a measure clearly supported by the town of Gandia), while all the time the effective status of the lesser nobility in Valencia continued to shrink before the growing influence of the rich and powerful merchants, many of whom were already 'honourable citizens' and for all practical purposes at a comparable social level to that of the knights (March attacks one of them in poem XLII). March was one of the local landowners responsible for developing the cultivation of sugarcane (and he built a mill to extract the sugar himself). His entire life seems to have been plagued by lawsuits, many of them instigated by him. There are written challenges to other knights over matters of honour and over money (such challenges were often a short-cut through a ponderous legal system), while the final years of his life were overcast by the accusation of incitement to the unprovoked attack on an old enemy as well as incitement to two murders, and the committing of another by his own hand. Because of these accusations he was imprisoned (released after one day on the Queen's command) and then put under house arrest (thanks again to the intervention of the Queen).

March married twice. The first wife, Isabel Martorell, was the sister of Joanot Martorell, author of the great Catalan chivalresque romance, *Tirant lo Blanc*. The wedding was much delayed because of an insufficient dowry which could only be made up once Joanot returned from his journey to the English court where he had gone to ask the king to settle a matter of honour; the marriage involved the expansion of March's seigneurial lands. Due to the delay, March seems to have wanted to withdraw from the arrangement, but was held to it by the Martorells. There are interesting documents that describe March's frequent visits to the betrothed, always in the company of his squires and servants. But the marriage ended less than a year later, in 1439, when Isabel died. His second marriage to Joana Escorna in 1443 lasted ten or eleven years (she died in 1453 or 1454) and also brought a rich dowry with it. March's will testifies to the high regard in which he held both wives, but especially Joana. Neither wife gave him an heir, but, as was normal with men of his class (and he had a relatively short married life), several illegitimate children were born to March both by free women and by slaves; one of these children was to be made his heir, but died before this could happen.

He died in 1459 in Valencia after an illness. Among his small collection of manuscript books (we have to assume that his main library, which assuredly included the quite extensive one of his father, was in Gandia or Beniarjó), two unbound volumes 'with verses' are mentioned. It is just conceivable that what is described here is the original manuscript, now lost, of his life's work as a poet.[12]

[12] The main sources for March's life are: Amédée Pagès, *Auzias March et ses prédécesseurs. Essai sur la poésie amoureuse et philosophique en Catalogne aux XIVe et XVe siècles* (Paris: Champion, 1912; reprint Geneva: Slatkine, 1974), and Jaume Chiner Gimeno, *Ausiàs March i la València del segle XV (1400-1459)* (Valencia: Generalitat Valenciana-Consell Valencià de Cultura, 1997).

LOVE POEMS

I

Així com cell qui en lo somni·s delita
e son delit de foll pensament ve,
ne pren a mi: que·l temps passat me té
4   l'imaginar, que altre bé no hi habita,
sentint estar en aguait ma dolor,
sabent de cert que en ses mans he de jaure.
Temps d'avenir en negun bé·m pot caure;
8   ço que és no-res a mi és lo millor.

Del temps passat me trob en gran amor,
amant no-res pus és ja tot finit.
D'aquest pensar me sojorn e·m delit,
12   mas quan lo perd, s'esforça ma dolor:
sí com aquell qui és jutjat a mort
e de llong temps la sap e s'aconhorta,
e creure·l fan que li serà estorta,
16   e·l fan morir sens un punt de record.

Plagués a Déu que mon pensar fos mort
e que passàs ma vida en dorment.
Malament viu qui té son pensament
20   per enemic, fent-li d'enuigs report,
e com lo vol d'algun plaer servir
li'n pren així com dona ab son infant
que, si verí li'n demana plorant,
24   ha tan poc seny que no·l sap contradir.

Fóra millor ma dolor soferir
que no mesclar poca part de plaer
entre aquells mals qui·m giten de saber.
28   Com del pensat plaer me cové eixir,
las!, mon delit dolor se converteix,
dobla's l'afany aprés d'un poc repòs:
sí co·l malalt que per un plasent mos
32   tot son menjar en dolor se nodreix;

I

I'M LIKE A MAN who spends his life in dreams,
whose only joy is what such folly holds,
for all my thoughts are captive to the past,
and only there for me can pleasure lie;   4
yet pain, I can be sure, just bides its time:
it lurks, and I will fall into its grasp.
The future holds no promise, not for me.
The best is what is over and is gone.   8

Call me a man enamoured of the past,
of what is nothing, and exists no more.
Memories are my solace and my joy;
but once they fade, then pain strikes sharply back.   12
Just so, a man might await the gallows,
with resignation comforting his soul;
then comes false news that his life will be spared
–and they take him and hang him, unprepared.   16

If only God would paralyse my brain
so I could spend a lifetime lost in sleep!
A wretch he is indeed whose thoughts become
the enemy, and his own mind torment,   20
and every time he looks to them for joy,
he's like a woman with her screaming child:
if it should ask with poison to be fed,
she can't refuse, she has so little sense.   24

I had best resign myself to simple pain,
forget all hope of mixing in some joy,
and let the torment take its fatal course.
Alas!, each time my dreams I set aside,   28
so suffering comes to take the place of joy;
a brief respite, and then redoubled pain:
the tasty morsel tempts the sickly man,
and then he must eat every meal in pain;   32

com l'ermità qui enyorament no·l creix
d'aquells amics que havia en lo món,
essent llong temps que en lloc poblat no fon,
36 fortuït cas un d'ells li apareix
qui los passats plaers li renovella,
sí que·l passat present li fa tornar,
mas com se'n part, l'és forçat congoixar.
40 Lo bé com fuig ab grans crits mal apella.

Tornada

Plena de seny, quan amor és molt vella,
absença és lo verme que la gasta,
si fermetat durament no contrasta,
44 e creure poc si l'envejós consella.

so is it for the hermit in his cave,
who over time has ceased to miss his friends
—the many that he left behind in town—
but one of them quite suddenly appears,   36
and all the former pleasures are recalled,
and past fills all the present once again;
the friend's farewell must usher in regret:
when good takes flight, it loudly summons pain.   40

Envoi

Beauteous Wisdom, whenever love grows old,
then absence chumbles at it like a worm;
constancy will starve it; this, and if you'll give
no heed to what these envious tongues might say.   44

II

Pren-me enaixí com al patró que en plaja
té sa gran nau e pensa haver castell.
Veent lo cel ésser molt clar e bell,
4   creu fermament d'una àncora assats haja.
E sent venir sobtós un temporal
de tempestat e temps incomportable.
Lleva son jui: que si molt és durable,
8   cercar los ports més que aturar li val.

Moltes veus és que·l vent és fortunal,
tant que no pot sortir sens lo contrari.
E cella clau que us tanca dins l'armari
12   no pot obrir aquell mateix portal.
Així m'ha pres, trobant-me enamorat,
per sobresalt qui·m ve de vós, ma aimia.
Del no amar desalt ne té la via,
16   mas un sol pas meu no hi serà trobat.

Menys que lo peix és en lo bosc trobat
e los lleons dins l'aigua han llur sojorn,
la mia amor per null temps pendrà torn,
20   sol coneixent que de mi us doneu grat.
E fiu de vós que·m sabreu bé conéixer
e, conegut, no·m serà mal graïda
tota dolor havent per vós sentida.
24   Lladoncs veureu les flames d'amor créixer!

Si mon voler he dat mal a aparéixer
creeu de cert que vera amor no·m lluny.
Pus que lo sol és cald al mes de juny
28   ard mon cor flac sens algun grat meréixer.
Altre, sens mi, d'açò mereix la colpa.
Vullau-li mal com tan humil servent
vos té secret per son defalliment.
32   Cest és amor que mi, amant, encolpa.

II

I AM LIKE the master of some great ship
riding at anchor off a stretch of beach,
who sees above a blue and cloudless sky:
a castle, he thinks, could not be safer.   4
All at once a storm he feels upon him,
and winds so strong it can't be weathered out.
The decision's made: now the storm sets in,
he must cast off, for some safe harbour try.   8

But often he is up against a gale
and can't get clear without a contrary wind
(for the key that locks you in the closet
is not the same as lets you out again).   12
Such, beloved lady, is the bind I'm in:
the exceeding joy that you alone afford
I must renounce, if love's to have an end;
but that's one path that I shall never tread.   16

Sooner say that fish are swimming in the wood
or that lions now across the oceans roam
than that my love can ever start to wane
–if only I am sure I don't displease you.   20
I believe that you will come to know me
for myself, and, when you do, ingratitude
will cease to be your answer to my pain.
Then will you see the flames of love's fire blaze!   24

If I have kept my feelings to myself,
it's not, be sure, because I lack true love.
My ailing heart burns hotter than the sun
in June, yet unrewarded it remains.   28
It's another's doing that this is so,
not mine; blame him who has failed to ensure
your humble servant's service reached your ears.
It's love that makes me love, then blames me too!   32

Ma voluntat ab la raó s'envolpa,
e fan acord, la qualitat seguint,
tals actes fent que·l cos és defallint
en poc de temps una gran part de polpa.
Lo poc dormir magresa al cos m'acosta;
dobla'm l'enginy per contemplar amor.
Lo cos molt gras, trobant-se dormidor,
no pot dar pas en aquesta aspra costa.

Tornada

Plena de seny, donau-me una crosta
del vostre pa qui·m lleve l'amargor.
De tot menjar m'ha pres gran dessabor
sinó d'aquell qui molta amor me costa.

In me desire and reason intertwine,
and in the love of spirit are as one,
so working together that my body
has shed the greater part of bulk; my flesh   36
is wasted from so many sleepless nights;
my sharpened wits can meditate on love.
To sleep all day is what fat bodies want;
up this steep slope they cannot take one step.   40

Envoi

Beauteous Wisdom, of your bread one crust
I ask, to take this bitterness away.
Intolerable is all food to me
excepting that which my great love may earn.   44

III

Alt e amor, d'on gran desig s'engendra,
e esper, vinent per tots aquests graons,
me són delits, mas dóna'm passions
la por del mal, qui·m fa magrir carn tendra,
e port al cor sens fum continu foc,
e la calor no·m surt a part de fora.
Socorreu-me dins los térmens d'una hora,
car mos senyals demostren viure poc!

Metge escient no té lo cas per joc
com la calor no surt a part extrema.
L'ignorant veu que lo malalt no crema
e jutja'l sa puis que mostra bon toc.
Lo pacient no porà dir son mal,
tot afeblit, ab llengua mal diserta.
Gests e color assats fan descoberta
part de l'afany, que tant com lo dir val.

Tornada

Plena de seny, dir-vos que us am no cal,
puis crec de cert que us ne teniu per certa,
si bé mostrau que us està molt coberta
cella perquè amor és desegual.

III

PLEASURE, LOVE, the fierce desire these beget,
hope that bears me from one stage to the next:
these bring but joy, yet fear of failure turns
it all to torment, and wastes my tender flesh,   4
while I feed a fire deep raging in my heart,
such that it gives off neither smoke nor heat.
Come to my rescue before this hour is done,
for this can only mean my imminent death!   8

A skilled physician always is alarmed
when he finds heat within the body trapped;
only a quack, finding there no fever
and no sweats, would then conclude that all was well.   12
For even if the patient's weak and frail,
and cannot put his symptoms into words,
then gestures, anguish, and his complexion,
can say, all three, as much as speaking will.   16

Envoi

Beauteous Wisdom, to say I love you
there's no need: I'm sure that you're quite sure of it,
show as you may you've not the slightest clue
why some might see imbalance in this love.   20

IV

Així com cell qui desija vianda
per apagar sa perillosa fam,
e veu dos poms de fruit en un bell ram
4   e son desig egualment los demanda,
no·l complirà fins part haja elegida
sí que·l desig vers l'un fruit se decant:
així m'ha pres dues dones amant.
8   Mas elegesc per haver d'amor vida.

Sí com la mar se plany greument e crida
com dos forts vents la baten egualment,
u de llevant e altre de ponent,
12   e dura tant fins l'un vent l'ha jaquida
sa força gran per lo més poderós,
dos grans desigs han combatut ma pensa
mas lo voler vers u seguir dispensa.
16   Jo·l vos public: amar dretament vós.

E no cuideu que tan innocent fos
que no veés vostre avantatge gran.
Mon cos no cast estava congoixant
20   de perdre lloc qui l'era delitós.
Una raó fon ab ell de sa part
dient que en ell se pren aquesta amor,
sentint lo mal o lo delit major,
24   sí que, ell content, cascú pot ésser fart.

L'enteniment a parlar no venc tard
e planament desféu esta raó,
dient que·l cos ab sa complexió
28   ha tal amor com un llop o renard
que llur poder d'amar és limitat,
car no és pus que apetit brutal,
e si l'amant veeu dins la fornal,
32   no serà plant e molt menys defensat.

IV

LIKE THE STARVING man on the brink of death,
who must find food or be prepared to die,
then sees two fruits that hang from one fine branch,
with equal longing wants to have them both,   4
but cannot eat until he's made his choice,
and fixes his desire on one alone,
thus I, who love two women equally.
But I will choose that love which gives me life.   8

Just as the sea will loudly groan and howl
when whipped with equal force by contrary winds,
one blowing from the west, the other east
–the struggle ceasing when the one gives way   12
before the greater might of the other wind–
so two desires have battled in my mind,
but now at last my will has made its choice.
Lady, it is this: to love you as I ought.   16

But do not think this means that I am blind
to those great gifts with which your person's graced;
this lewd body has fretted long to think
that it must lose such promise of delight.   20
One argument it had to make its case,
saying that the body's where such love is born,
and where its pain is felt and its delight;
no form of love can flourish while it yearns.   24

The understanding promptly made reply,
and soon made nonsense of the body's words,
and said that, by its very nature, flesh
thinks of love as a wolf does, or a fox,   28
who naturally no higher can aspire
than will their bestial appetite allow,
and if in love's furnace we see lovers burn,
no pity they deserve, much less defence.   32

Ell és qui venç la sensualitat.
Si bé no és en ell prim moviment,
en ell està de tot lo jutjament:
36   cert guiador és de la voluntat.
¿Qui és aquell qui en contra d'ell reny?
Que voluntat, per qui·l fet s'executa,
l'atorg senyor, e si ab ell disputa
40   a la perfí se guia per son seny.

Diu més avant al cos ab gran endeny:
«Vanament vols, e vans són tos desigs,
car dins un punt tos delits són fastigs;
44   romans-ne llas: tot jorn ne prens enseny.
Ab tu mateix delit no pots haver:
tant est grosser que amor no n'és servit.
Volenterós acte de bé és dit,
48   e d'aquest bé tu no saps lo carrer.

Si bé complit lo món pot retener,
per mi és l'hom en tan sobiran bé.
E qui sens mi esperança·l reté
52   és foll o pec e terrible grosser.»
Aitant com és l'enteniment pus clar
és gran delit lo que per ell se pren.
E son pillard és subtil pensament,
56   qui de fins pasts no·l jaqueix endurar.

Tornada

Plena de seny, no pot Déu a mi dar
fora de vós que descontent no camp.
Tots mos desigs sobre vós los escamp;
60   tot és dins vós lo que·m fa desijar.

Sensuality always it defeats;
in desire's first impulse it has no part,
but it alone can judgement exercise,
and thereby be the will's unfailing guide.   36
The understanding cannot be denied.
The will, through which all actions are performed,
calls it master and, though it may dissent,
by reason will be governed in the end.   40

More it has to say, indignant, to the flesh:
'Vain are all your hopes, and vain are your desires:
no sooner have you sampled your delights
you're bored and flaccid: you will never learn.   44
Unaided, you're incapable of pleasure,
too brutish to be of service to love;
an act of the will to attain a good
is love; but you've no clue where such good lies.   48

If good, absolute, can in this life be found,
then only through me may such good be known.
Who without my help aspires to reach it
is mad, or else a fool, or mindless lout.'   52
A lucid understanding is the only way
that we may attain the higher pleasures;
always it rides with subtle thought at hand,
sustaining it ever with the choicest foods.   56

Envoi

Beauteous Wisdom, if not you, there's nothing
I'd ask of God to make me once content.
All my desires I've cast on you alone,
and in you alone such desires take shape.   60

V

Tant he amat que mon grosser enginy
per gran treball de pensa és subtil.
Lleixant a part aquell sentiment vil
4   que en jorn present los enamorats ciny,
só tan sabent que sé ben departir
amor d'aquell desig no virtuós;
car tot desig retent hom congoixós
8   no és vera amor ne per tal se deu dir.

Així com Déu si no·l plac descobrir
estant enclòs en lo virginal ventre,
e quan isqué defora d'aquell centre
12   mai lo Satan lo poc ben discernir,
ans, quan en ell veia·l cos de natura,
creia de cert aquell no ésser Déu,
mas ja retut son esperit en creu,
16   sabé·l mester que paradís procura:

per mals parlers, he tret saber e cura
de retenir lo foc d'amor sens fum,
e per açò he cartejat volum
20   d'aquell saber que sens amor no dura.
Viscut he molt sens ésser conegut
per molts senyals que fictes he mostrats,
mas quan seré per hom foll publicats,
24   serà ben cert lo tard apercebut.

Sia en vós aitant de bé caigut,
obrant en vós arreglada mercé,
que veent-mi despullat de tot bé,
28   no·m despreeu pel dan a mi vengut.
E si per vós he nom de foll atés
e contra mi só restat malmirent,
sia per vós cregut savi sabent
32   puis que per vós mon seny hauré despés.

V

LONG AND HARD for love my mind has laboured,
honing and sharpening my once dull wit.
I scorn those base feelings that in present
times lovers each unto the other bind;   4
my understanding's such that I can tell
true love from every other low desire;
for such are not all those desires that come
to torment lovers, and such should not be called.   8

Just as God chose to hide himself away,
enclosing his Godhead in the Virgin's womb,
and once he departed that holy place,
Satan could never tell that it was He,   12
but saw instead the body of a man,
sure in his certainty it was not God,
until Christ rendered, crucified, his soul,
and learnt only then of paradise regained,   16

so evil tongues mean all my skill and wit
must hide the smoke that issues from love's fire,
and I have scoured the pages of that book
that speaks of wisdom only love sustains.   20
For long, undetected, have I lived this way,
fooling the world with my misleading signs;
but by the time they'll certify me mad,
I will have more than justified that name.   24

My only hope is that you may possess
such good, in equal measure pity too,
that when you see me stripped of every boon,
you'll not despise me for my wretchedness;   28
and if –because of you– they call me mad,
and I even come to despise myself,
say only you'll pronounce me to be wise,
since all my wits were spent for love of you.   32

Si per amar a vós, havia atés
honor e béns, bellea i saviesa,
l'amor que us he tendria per ofesa
36   si tal semblant en vós no paregués.
Ma voluntat en si tal càrrec porta
que no serà sens la vostra contenta,
e per null cas me pens que no dissenta
40   que null desig li sodegue la porta.

Tornada

Plena de seny, natura no·m comporta
que tal dolor no descresca ma vida.
Si Déu pregàs, ma veu seria oïda.
44   Oïu-la vós, pus veritat reporta.

Even if my love for you had brought me
wisdom and honour and beauty and wealth,
I could not be satisfied until I saw
in you true signs of love to match my own.   36
Desire like mine can never rest content
until the day that you reciprocate;
of this I'm certain: all other desires
that even try the door will get short shrift.   40

Envoi

Beauteous Wisdom, where there's pain like mine,
Nature can do nothing to stop my death.
God would hear, if I asked his help, my prayers.
Listen, then: I tell you nothing but the truth.   44

VII

Sí com rictat no porta béns ab si,
mas val aitant com cell qui n'és senyor,
amor no val mas tant com l'amador:
manxa bufant orgue fals no ret fi.
Amor val poc com tot enamorat
ha falsedat en son pits fals enclosa,
o és ajunt ab una tal esposa:
peguea és son dret nom apellat.

Amor no pot haver desordenat
ço que Déus fa, natura mijançant,
car home pec no pot ser fin amant,
ne lo subtil contra sa qualitat.
Mal pendrà pinta en l'aigua sa figura:
molt menys amor pendrà lo no dispost;
ne pot estar l'aigua dins un lloc rost:
així amor en cap d'hom foll atura.

Per ben amar ab angoixosa cura
en temps passat eren lladoncs volguts.
Ovidi·l prous dix que amor és crescuts
per altra amor demostrant sa factura.
Verdader fon son dit e sos presics
tant quant amor fon prop de coneixença,
mas en est cas entre ells ha malvolença,
tal que no creu null temps sien amics.

Si fóssem nats vós e jo entre·ls antics,
lai quan amor amant se conqueria,
sens praticar alguna maestria,
lo vostre cor no fóra tan inics.
En vós conec gran disposició
de fer tot ço que gentilea mana,
mas criament veig que natura engana,
car viure ab mals és d'hom perdició.

VII

JUST AS RICHES hold no value in themselves,
but what their owner makes them, nothing more,
so love is as good as the one who loves:
bellows there's none can make a faulty organ   4
give clear notes; love can be of little worth
when lovers harbour falseness in their breasts
or else come close to making it their bride.
Then love has changed to plain stupidity.   8

What God through Nature does, love cannot undo;
and thus no fool will make a sensitive
lover, nor may even the subtlest wits
their natural limitations overcome.   12
Sooner paint portraits on the running stream
than ask love favour those who are not apt,
and even less can water gather on a slope
than ever love in foolish heads reside.   16

Gone is the time when suffering, devotion,
still were rewarded with requited love.
It needed only, noble Ovid said,
that love were true, to grow in the beloved.   20
Everything he wrote and preached of love
held good while men still knew what true love was,
but in this age we see it so despised,
I doubt that love and men can be at peace.   24

Had we been born, we two, in days of old,
when love, merely by loving, was secured,
and lovers had no need to use love's wiles,
your heart with me would not be half so cruel.   28
Everything that I perceive in you
speaks of nobility and worthy deeds,
but nurture among men our nature hides;
evil surrounds us; by this we're undone.   32

Per mal grair ne per mala saó
mon cor no pot amor desemparar.
Devotament los me plau remembrar
36   aquells passats, a qui don Déus perdó;
e com seré traspassat d'aquest món,
lletres diran sobre la mia tomba:
«Plena de seny, no tingau a gran bomba
40   car per vós muir e vaig no sabent on».

Enveja és tal que tot primer confon
a tots aquells qui ab si la s'ajusten:
los envejats un poc ne molt no gusten
44   aquell mal tast que·ls envejosos fon.
Tal és amor, car jo qui la m'ajust
sent grans dolors, dant-me folls moviments,
e vós haveu d'açò tals sentiments
48   com fort destral ha de tallar molt fust.

Sí com Adam pres mal del vedat gust
com sa muller li mostrà mal camí,
dient 'Adam, mengem d'aquest bocí
52   e semblarem a Déu qui és tot just',
ne pren a mi, car mon seny ha cregut
la voluntat, fent-li promissió
que, ben servint, aconsegria do
56   que per null temps tal no fon conegut.

Per mal servir no crec l'haja perdut,
car si·ls treballs hagués soferts per Déu,
cos gloriós fóra en lo regne seu;
60   e ja plorant, sovint me trobe mut.
Si·m fos donat aquest temps en entendre
los grans secrets enclosos en natura,
no fóra al món cosa que·m fos escura,
64   dels fets divins gran part ne pogra atendre.

Tornada

Plena de seny, tot mon seny vull despendre
amant a vós, sens algun grat cossegre,
e durarà fins que del riu de Segre
68   l'aigua corrent amunt se puga estendre.

Untimely is this love and thankless,
yet, even so, my heart will not let go.
I remember all those lovers from the past
—God rest their souls!— and think of them as saints;   36
and when it's time for me to leave this life
upon my tomb this motto be inscribed:
'Beauteous Wisdom, of this you should not boast:
for you I died, and go I know not where'.   40

Such is envy that, once it's taken root,
envious minds are cheated from the start:
completely unaware are the envied
of all those bitter thoughts that envy feeds.   44
Love is much the same; to love I've given way
only to let in madness and fierce pain;
and through it all I know you feel for me
much like an axe as it chops a pile of wood.   48

Adam knew evil once he took the bite
that God forbade him, led astray by Eve,
saying he should taste with her a morsel,
and like their maker so would both become;   52
thus it is with me: my understanding
gives credence to what the will has promised:
that its good service rich rewards will earn,
whose like was never equalled in the world.   56

Was it poor service lost her? That cannot be:
if for God I'd suffered all I have for her,
now in His realm a glorious form I'd be;
instead, I often cannot speak for tears.   60
If all this time I had again and spent it
studying secrets that in Creation lie,
the earth would hold no mysteries for me,
the deeds of God would be within my grasp.   64

                              Envoi

Beauteous Wisdom, all my understanding
to love you serves, with nothing in return;
Spain's great rivers shall start to flow upstream
before I'll ever waver from this course.   68

X

Sí COM UN REI, senyor de tres ciutats,
qui tot son temps l'ha plagut guerrejar
ab l'enemic, qui d'ell no·s pot vantar
4   mai lo vencés menys d'ésser-ne sobrats,
ans, si·l matí l'enemic lo vencia,
ans del sol post pel rei era vençut,
fins que en les hosts contra·l rei fon vengut
8   un soldader qui lo rei desconfia;

lladoncs lo rei perdé la senyoria
de les ciutats, sens ulla posseir,
mas l'enemic dues li'n volc jaquir,
12   dant fe lo rei que bon compte·n retria
com a vassall, la renda despenent
a voluntat del desposseïdor;
de l'altra vol que no·n sia senyor,
16   ne sia vist que li vinga en esment:

llong temps amor per enemic lo sent,
mas jamés fon que·m donàs un mal jorn,
que en poc instant no li fes pendre torn,
20   foragitant son aspre pensament;
tot m'ha vençut ab sol esforç d'un cos,
ne l'ha calgut mostrar sa potent força.
Los tres poders que en l'arma són me força;
24   dos me'n jaqueix, de l'altre usar no gos.

E no cuideu que·m sia plasent mos
aquest vedat, ans n'endure de grat;
si bé no puc remembrar lo passat,
28   molt és plasent la càrrega a mon dors.
Jamés vençó fon plaer del vençut
sinó de mi, que·m plau que amor me vença
e·m tinga pres ab sa invisible llença,
32   mas paren bé sos colps en mon escut.

X

COMPARE ME to this: a king with cities three,
content to spend his long years waging war
against an enemy who could not boast,
not even once, that he had won the day;   4
some mornings he might have the upper hand,
but was pushed back before the sun had set
–until the day a mercenary joined
the enemy, and he at last was crushed.   8

No more could he over all three cities
rule as lord: now not a single one he held;
yet the enemy granted him two to keep as his,
and the king swore to be his loyal thrall,   12
to answer to him in all their affairs,
to dispose of the income as the new lord wished,
entry forbidden to the third –and thoughts
of gaining power should never cross his mind.   16

For long I've had my enemy in love,
but if ever he began to win the day,
at once I pushed him into full retreat
and all his bitter thoughts have driven out.   20
But by one body now I'm quite undone,
and love has won the battle without force;
he has conquered all three powers of my soul,
leaving me two; I dare not the other use.   24

But I shall not pretend I really miss
what I'm forbidden: I'm glad to go without.
While I am free of memories now past,
happily I bear the load upon my back.   28
No one but I such pleasure ever took,
defeated, in captivity to love,
bound, content, by its invisible rope,
proud that my shield bears witness to his blows.   32

De fet que fui a sa mercé vengut,
l'enteniment per son conseller pres,
e mon voler per alguazir lo mes,
36   dant fe cascú que mai serà rebut
en sa mercé lo companyó membrar,
servint cascú llealment son ofici,
sí que algú d'ells no serà tan nici
40   que en res contrast que sia de amar.

Tornada

Plena de seny, vullau-vos acordar
com per amor vénen grans sentiments
e per amor pot ser hom innocents.
44   E mostre-ho jo, qui n'he perdut parlar.

Once at love's mercy, straight he appointed
my understanding as his counsellor,
and into his bailiff turned my will, each
swearing that never would he take pity   36
on memory, companion of the past,
loyally each his duties to perform,
never turning to those forms of folly
that might impede the exercise of love.   40

Envoi

Beauteous Wisdom, remember only this:
love inspires deep passions, that will render
useless everything that men know. Take me:
I have forgotten even how to speak.   44

XI

¿QUINS TAN SEGURS consells vas encercant,
cor malastruc, enfastijat de viure,
amic de plor e desamic de riure?
4 ¿Com soferràs los mals qui·t són davant?
Acuita't, doncs, a la mort qui t'espera.
E per tos mals te allongues los jorns:
aitant és lluny ton delitós sojorns
8 com vols fugir a la mort falaguera.

Braços oberts és eixida a carrera,
plorant sos ulls per sobres de gran goig.
Melodiós cantar de sa veu oig,
12 dient: «Amic, ix de casa estrangera!
En delit prenc donar-te ma favor,
que per null temps home nat l'ha sentida,
car jo defuig a tot home que·m crida,
16 prenent aquell qui fuig de ma rigor.»

Ab ulls plorants e cara de terror,
cabells rompent, ab grans udolaments,
la vida·m vol donar heretaments
20 e d'aquests dons vol que sia senyor,
cridant ab veu horrible i dolorosa
tal com la mort crida al benauirat
(car si l'hom és a mals aparellat,
24 la veu de mort li és melodiosa).

Bé·m maravell com és tan ergullosa
la voluntat de cascun amador,
no demanant a mi qui és amor:
28 en mi sabran sa força poderosa.
Tots, maldient, sagramentejaran
que mai amor los tendrà en son poder.
E si·ls recont l'acolorat plaer,
32 lo temps perdut sospirant maldiran.

XI

OH WRETCHED heart, why not admit it's hopeless?
You're sick of life, a friend to tears, averse
to laughter: where is there now for you to turn?
And how to bear the pain that lies ahead?   4
Here's my advice: go where Death awaits you;
hold onto life, and you'll prolong the pain:
the sweetness of rest stays ever out of reach
while you ignore the solaces of Death.   8

Arms spread in welcome, Death cuts across my path,
tears streaming from her eyes in utter joy.
I listen as she sings the sweetest song:
'Why do you not forsake this stranger's house?   12
To you my special favour, friend, I grant,
such that none in this world has ever known:
when men cry out to me, I turn away
and seize on those who try to flee my touch.'   16

Then Life screams out to me, and tears her hair,
horror written on her face, tears gushing
from her eyes. She offers to bequeath me
Life's estate, to make me lord of all she has,   20
and yet her chilling voice shrieks just as shrill
as Death who summons those whom Life had blessed
(the loveliest melodies that Death can sing
only the joyless wretch can ever hear).   24

How arrogant must other lovers be
who go to love, and feel no need to ask
of me what kind of force they're dealing with!
From me they'd learn the nature of his strength,   28
and they would all curse love and vow to God
that it will never hold them in its power;
from me they'd learn how false love's pleasures are,
and sigh, and damn their love for wasted years.   32

Null hom conec o dona mon semblant
que, dolorit per amor, faça plànyer.
Jo son aquell de qui·s deu hom complànyer,
36   car de mon cor la sang se'n va llunyant
per gran tristor que li és acostada.
Seca's tot jorn l'humit qui·m sosté vida,
e la tristor contra mi és ardida;
40   en mon socors mà no s'hi troba armada.

Tornada

Llir entre cards, l'hora sent acostada
que civilment és ma vida finida.
Puis que del tot ma esperança és fugida,
44   ma arma roman en aquest món damnada.

Many men I know, and women, whom love
torments, but none can be compared to me.
If anyone has ever earned pity,
then I have: the blood ebbs slow from a heart   36
weighed down by sadness, the vital liquid
that sustains my life day by day dries out,
bolder in its offensive sadness grows,
and I've no troops with which to make a stand.   40

Envoi

Lily among thorns, I feel the hour draw near
when my life among men will reach its end.
Abandoned by the little hope it had,
damned in this world my soul must now abide.   44

XIII

COLGUEN LES GENTS ab alegria festes,
lloant a Déu, entremesclant deports;
places, carrers e delitables horts
4   sien cercats, ab recont de grans gestes.
E vaja jo los sepulcres cercant,
interrogant ànimes infernades;
e respondran, car no són companyades
8   d'altre que mi en son continu plant.

Cascú requer e vol a son semblant;
per ço no·m plau la pràtica dels vius:
d'imaginar mon estat són esquius;
12   sí com d'hom mort de mi prenen espant.
Lo rei xipré, presoner d'un heretge,
en mon esguard no és malauirat,
car ço que vull no serà mai finat;
16   de mon desig no·m porà guarir metge.

Cell Teixion qui·l buitre·l menja·l fetge,
e per tots temps brota la carn de nou
e en son menjar aquell ocell mai clou:
20   pus fort dolor d'aquesta·m té lo setge,
car és un verm qui romp la mia pensa,
altre lo cor, qui mai cessen de rompre;
e llur treball no·s porà enterrompre
24   sinó ab ço que d'haver se defensa.

E si la mort no·m dugués tal ofensa
–fer mi absent d'una tan plasent vista–
no li graesc que de terra no vista
28   lo meu cos nu, qui de plaer no pensa
de perdre pus que lo imaginar
los meus desigs no poder-se complir.
E si·m cové mon darrer jorn finir,
32   seran donats térmens a ben amar.

XIII

WHY SHOULD I object if people only think
of feast-days, and how best to mix in fun
with worship, and fill the squares and streets
and bright gardens, and hear the great tales sung?   4
For I would sooner walk among the tombs
and ply damned spirits with my questions;
I know they'll answer, for there's no one else
who'd willingly join their lamentation.   8

Every creature craves its selfsame likeness;
that's why the ways of the living aren't for me;
I can't expect that others understand
what I suffer; like a corpse I scare them all.   12
Compared to me, that king of Cyprus, prisoner
of an infidel, had little to endure:
to my longing there will never be an end;
there's no physician can cure such desire.   16

More than for Tityos, as the vulture tears
his ever-replenished liver and in all
eternity will never end its meal,
far greater is the pain assailing me,   20
for while in my mind one worm gnaws constantly,
another feeds incessant on my heart.
And there is nothing that can make them stop
except the very thing I cannot have.   24

My death would just make matters worse, for then
on such loveliness as yours I couldn't gaze;
else my naked body I'd have death deck
with clods of earth, for I can count on nothing   28
pleasurable, and all my life is spent
brooding on desire for ever unfulfilled.
And no sooner shall my days be over
than also for true love the end will come.   32

E si en lo cel Déu me vol allogar,
part veure a Ell, per complir mon delit
serà mester que·m sia dellai dit
36   que d'esta mort vos ha plagut plorar,
penedint-vos com per poca mercé
mor l'innocent e per amar-vos martre,
cell qui lo cos de l'arma vol departre
40   si ferm cregués que us dolríeu de se.

Tornada

Llir entre cards, vós sabeu e jo sé
que·s pot bé fer hom morir per amor;
creure de mi que só en tal dolor
44   no fareu molt que hi doneu plena fe.

And if God should take me up to Heaven
and I beheld Him, even then my bliss
would only be complete if I was sure
that you had wept to learn that I was dead,   36
repentant that your cruel and ruthless heart
had martyred an innocent to your love,
one who willingly would render up his soul,
could he be sure you'd pity such a death.   40

     Envoi

Lily among thorns, you know as well as I
how easily a man may die of love.
Why should you doubt I've come to such a pass?
You've every cause to take me at my word.   44

XVIII

FANTASIANT, amor a mi descobre
los grans secrets que als pus subtils amaga,
e mon jorn clar als hòmens és nit fosca,
4 e visc de ço que persones no tasten.
Tant en amor l'esperit meu contempla
que par del tot fora del cos s'aparte,
car mos desigs no són trobats en home,
8 sinó en tal que la carn punt no·l torbe.

Ma carn no sent aquell desig sensible,
e l'esperit obres d'amor cobeja;
d'aquell cec foc qui·ls amadors s'escalfen
12 paor no·m trop que jo me'n pogués ardre.
Un altre esguard lo meu voler pratica
quan en amar-vos, dona, se contenta,
que no han cells qui amadors se mostren,
16 passionats e, contra amor, no dignes.

Si fos amor substança raonable,
e que·s trobàs de senyoria ceptre,
béns guardonant e punint los demèrits,
20 entre·ls mellors sols me trobara fènix,
car jo tot sols desempare la mescla
de lleigs desigs qui ab los bons s'embolquen.
Càstig no·m cal, puis de assaig no·m tempten;
24 la causa llur en mi és feta nul·la.

Sí com los sants, sentints la llum divina,
la llum del món conegueren per ficta,
e menyspreants la glòria mundana
28 puis major part de glòria sentien,
tot enaixí tinc en menyspreu e fàstig
aquells desigs qui, complits, amor minva,
prenint aquells que de l'esperit mouen,
32 qui no és llassat, ans tot jorn muntiplica.

XVIII

In reveries has love revealed to me
deep secrets hid from men of subtler wit;
clear day for me is others' darkest night,
sustained by food which they can never taste.   4
So deeply does my spirit ponder love,
it rises up, the body left behind;
none can aspire to know desires like mine,
unless he's quite untroubled by the flesh.   8

My body is untouched by lewd desires;
alone for acts of love the spirit longs;
I have no fear that I could be consumed
by that blind fire with which most lovers burn.   12
With other ends my will is bent on love
of you, lady, and with other joys than
those lovers self-proclaimed, to passions bound,
unworthy, and the enemies of love.   16

If love were substance, and with reason crowned,
wielding the sceptre of its sovereignty,
rewarding good works, punishing misdeeds,
among the best a phoenix I would be: 20
I disentangle –only I– the skein
of good desires that reach man mixed with foul.
By these untouched, I'm quite beyond reproach;
in me their cause can only ever fail.   24

Just as the saints, perceiving Heaven's light,
saw at once the falseness of this world's light,
and then much greater glory they discerned
when worldly glories they had learnt to scorn,   28
in just this way, I loathe and I abhor
desires which, satisfied, then leave love dead;
only those I choose that from the spirit rise,
that never fails, but ever stronger grows.   32

Sí com sant Pau Déu li sostragué l'arma
del cos perquè ves divinals misteris
(car és lo cos de l'esperit lo carçre,
36   e tant com viu ab ell és en tenebres),
així amor l'esperit meu arrapa,
e no hi acull la maculada pensa.
E per ço sent lo delit qui no·s cansa,
40   sí que ma carn la vera amor no·m torba.

Pren-me enaixí com aquell filosofe
qui, per muntar al bé qui no·s pot perdre,
los perdedors llançà en mar profunda,
44   creent aquells l'enteniment torbassen:
jo, per muntar al delit perdurable
(tant quant ha·l món), gros plaer de mi llance,
creent de cert que·l gran delit me torba
48   aquell plaer que en fàstig, volant, passa.

Als naturals no par que fer se pusquen
molts dels secrets que la deitat s'estoja,
que revelats són estats a molts martres
52   no tan subtils com los ignorants i aptes;
així primors amor a mi revela,
tals que·ls sabents no basten a compendre;
e quan ho dic, de mos dits me desmenten,
56   dant a parer que folles coses parle.

Tornada

Llir entre cards, lo meu voler se tempra
en ço que null amador sap lo tempre.
Ço fai amor, a qui plau que jo senta
60   sos grans tresors; sols a mi·ls manifesta.

As when God drew Paul's spirit from the flesh,
that he might holy mysteries perceive
(the spirit dungeoned in the body lies,
and dwelling there, it can but darkness know),   36
in such a way love bears my spirit off,
but will not touch a single tainted thought.
Unfading pleasure thus is mine, and flesh
cannot impede the workings of pure love.   40

Like that philosopher I'd say I am
who, striving for the good that never ends,
cast all his worldly goods into the sea,
the encumbrance to his understanding: 44
in just this way I strive for lasting joy
(as much as this world holds), casting aside
all gross delights, for true joy cannot lie
in fleeting pleasures that in loathing end.   48

The natural philosophers deny
that many secrets kept from us by God
should to numerous martyrs be revealed
and yet be hidden from cleverer men,   52
just so, love lends to me such subtle truths
even the wisest cannot comprehend;
and if I speak of them, they say I lie,
and that I utter not one word of sense.   56

Envoi

Lily among thorns, of such stuff my will
is forged as no other lover's has been cast.
Love so chose to make me: its vast treasures
alone to share, revealed to none but me.   60

XXVIII

Lo jorn ha por de perdre sa claror
quan ve la nit que expandeix ses tenebres.
Pocs animals no cloen les palpebres
4 e los malalts creixen de llur dolor;
los malfactors volgren tot l'any duràs
perquè llurs mals haguessen cobriment;
mas jo, qui visc menys de par en turment
8 e sens mal fer, volgra que tost passàs.

E d'altra part faç pus que si matàs
mil hòmens justs menys d'alguna mercé,
car tots mos ginys jo solt per trair-me.
12 E no cuideu que·l jorn me n'excusàs,
ans, en la nit treball rompent ma pensa
perquè en lo jorn lo traïment cometa.
Por de morir o de fer vida estreta
16 no·m tol esforç per donar-me ofensa.

Tornada

Plena de seny, mon enteniment pensa
com aptament lo llaç d'amor se meta.
Sens aturar, pas tenint via dreta.
20 Vaig a la fi si mercé no·m defensa.

XXVIII

DAY SEES WITH terror how its last light fades
and night comes, spreading darkness in its path.
Wide-eyed, small creatures dare not welcome sleep;
the sick and weak endure redoubled pain.   4
Now evil men come out to do their worst:
cloaked by the dark, they'd have it last all year.
Not I: of me need none fear harm, tormented
like no other: I long for night to pass.   8

And yet, if I had murdered a thousand
guiltless men I could do no worse: each night
I set my wits to plot my betrayal.
And don't suppose the dawn will bring respite: 12
all night I'm busy wrenching from my mind
how best to shape the next day's perfidy.
What fear holds death or else the prison cell
in one who's traitor to his very self?   16

Envoi

Beauteous Wisdom, there's none to blame but me
if Love has placed his noose around my neck.
The road runs straight, and I don't drag my steps.
The end's in sight: will pity send reprieve?   20

XXIX

Sí com lo taur se'n va fuit pel desert
quan és sobrat per son semblant qui·l força,
ne torna mai fins ha cobrada força
per destruir aquell qui l'ha desert,   4
tot enaixí·m cové llunyar de vós
car vostre gest mon esforç ha confús.
No tornaré fins del tot haja fus
la gran paor qui·m tol ser delitós.   8

XXIX

DEEP IN THE wilderness the wild bull flees,
the fierce battle lost with one of his kind,
but once he's built up strength, goes straight to seek
him out, and with defeat avenge his loss;   4
such am I, who for my own good flee you:
your beauty was enough to sap my strength.
I'll not return until I've quelled the fear
that stands between me and all chance of joy.   8

XXXIX

QUI NO ÉS TRIST, de mos dictats no cur,
o en algun temps que sia trist estat;
e lo qui és de mals passionat,
per fer-se trist, no cerque lloc escur;
llija mos dits, mostrants pensa torbada,
sens alguna art eixits d'hom fora seny.
E la raó que en tal dolor m'empeny
amor ho sap, qui n'és causa estada.

Alguna part, e molta, és trobada
de gran delit en la pensa del trist,
e si les gents ab gran dolor m'han vist,
de gran delit ma arma fon companyada.
Quan simplement amor en mi habita,
tal delit sent que no·m cuid ser al món,
e com sos fets vull veure de pregon,
mescladament ab dolor me delita.

Prest és lo temps que faré vida ermita,
per mills poder d'amor les festes colre;
d'est viure estrany algú no·s vulla dolre,
car per sa cort amor me vol e·m cita.
E jo qui l'am per si tan solament,
no denegant lo do que pot donar,
a sa tristor me plau abandonar,
e per tostemps viure entristadament.

Traure no pusc de mon enteniment
que sia cert e molt pus bell partit
sa tristor gran que tot altre delit,
puis hi recau delitós llanguiment.
Alguna part de mon gran delit és
aquella que tot home trist aporta:
que, planyent si, lo plànyer lo conforta
més que si d'ell tot lo món se dolgués.

XXXIX

ONLY SAD LOVERS, or who once were such,
need bother reading anything I write;
but those of you whose lives are shot with pain
don't drag your sadness off to some dark hole: 4
just read my poems, full of frenzied thoughts,
a madman's ravings, without the aid of art.
And why am I forced to live in such distress?
That only love can know, whose fault it is.   8

Intense delight, and in no small measure,
awaits the man who thinks the saddest thoughts;
even when others have seen me in great pain,
this great pleasure has comforted my soul.   12
When simply I let love within me dwell,
such is my delight that to the world I'm lost,
but once I try to understand its ways,
then pain begins to mingle with delight.   16

Soon I'll go off to lead the hermit's life,
the better all love's feast-days to observe;
no need to pity such strange behaviour:
to attend his court has love summoned me.   20
While love for itself I love and revere
(though I'd not scorn the gift that it might make),
with just its sadness I'll content myself,
sadly to spend each moment of the day.   24

There's one thing I cannot help believing:
finer by far is the sadness love brings
than all other joy, and much to be preferred,
since the lover may languish, yet still feel delight.   28
Part of my sad pleasure little differs
from what through sadness any man may know:
he pities his own plight, and this comforts more
than if the whole world had joined in his lament.   32

Ésser me cuid per moltes gents représ,
puis que tant llou viure en la vida trista,
mas jo, qui he sa glòria a l'ull vista,
36   desig sos mals, puis delit hi és promés.
No·s pot saber, menys de l'experiença,
lo gran delit que és en lo sols voler
d'aquell qui és amador verdader,
40   e ama si, veent-se en tal volença.

Tornada

Llir entre cards, Déu vos don coneixença
com só per vós a tot extrem posat:
ab mon poder amor m'ha enderrocat,
44   sens aquell seu d'infinida potença.

Many will take exception, I've no doubt,
that I should praise the life in sadness lived,
but I've seen its glory with my own eyes:
I want its pain for the pleasure it affords.   36
One must feel it to be able to sense
what great delight, merely by loving,
awaits him who knows truly how to love,
and with his own desires has come to terms.   40

Envoi

Lily among thorns, would to God you'd see
I'm pulled to one extreme and then the next;
love with my strength alone has thrown me down,
holding in reserve its infinite power.   44

XLVI

VELES E VENTS han mos desigs complir
faent camins dubtosos per la mar.
Mestre i ponent contra d'ells veig armar:
xaloc, llevant los deuen subvenir
ab llurs amics lo grec e lo migjorn,
fent humils precs al vent tramuntanal
que en son bufar los sia parcial
e que tots cinc complesquen mon retorn.

Bullirà·l mar com la cassola en forn,
mudant color e l'estat natural,
e mostrarà voler tota res mal
que sobre si atur un punt al jorn.
Grans e pocs peixs a recors correran
e cercaran amagatalls secrets;
fugint al mar on són nodrits e fets,
per gran remei en terra eixiran.

Los pelegrins tots ensems votaran
e prometran molts dons de cera fets;
la gran paor traurà al llum los secrets
que al confés descoberts no seran.
En lo perill no·m caureu de l'esment,
ans votaré al Déu qui·ns ha lligats
de no minvar mes fermes voluntats
e que tots temps me sereu de present.

Jo tem la mort per no ser-vos absent,
perquè amor per mort és anul·lats;
mas jo no creu que mon voler sobrats
pusca esser per tal departiment.
Jo só gelós de vostre escàs voler
que, jo morint, no meta mi en oblit.
Sol est pensar me tol del món delit
car, nós vivint, no creu se pusca fer:

XLVI

I SHALL RETURN: the winds shall swell my sails,
I'll set a course of danger through the sea,
not caring West and North-West winds take arms:
Levanter with Sirocco will hold firm,   4
helped by their allies –North-Eastern, Midi–
who humbly will entreat the great North wind
to stay its blasts, so favouring their cause
that all five together may bring me back.   8

The sea shall bubble like a pot of stew,
losing its form and colour as it seethes.
All that upon it a single moment
ventures will feel its malice at full force,   12
and all the creatures of the deep in vain
will rush to seek some secret refuge, fleeing
the very sea which spawned and nurtured them,
on dry land leaping to their desperate end.   16

The pilgrims all as one will make their vows,
pledging their offerings of votive wax,
and sheer terror will force those secrets out
that never fell on the confessor's ear.   20
In such danger, you shall not leave my thoughts,
and to the God who joined us I shall vow
never to weaken in my firm resolve,
and day and night to only think of you.   24

I fear death, that is eternal absence
and by which love is always cancelled out,
not that I believe such parting –even this–
could overcome the strength of my desire.   28
I long for you to love me as you should,
and that you'll not forget me if I died.
But one thought there is that makes me wretched
(and this could never be while we two live):   32

aprés ma mort d'amar perdau poder
e sia tost en ira convertit,
e jo, forçat d'aquest món ser eixit,
36   tot lo meu mal serà vós no veer.
Oh Déu, ¿per què terme no hi ha en amor,
car prop d'aquell jo·m trobara tot sol?
Vostre voler sabera quant me vol,
40   tement, fiant, de tot l'avenidor.

Jo són aquell pus extrem amador
aprés d'aquell a qui Déu vida tol.
Puis jo són viu, mon cor no mostra dol
44   tant com la mort per sa extrema dolor.
A bé o mal d'amor jo só dispost,
mas per mon fat fortuna cas no·m porta.
Tot esvetlat, ab desbarrada porta,
48   me trobarà faent humil respost.

Jo desig ço que·m porà ser gran cost
i aquest esper de molts mals m'aconhorta.
A mi no plau ma vida ser estorta
52   d'un cas molt fer, qual prec Déu sia tost;
lladoncs les gents no·ls calrà donar fe
al que amor fora mi obrarà;
lo seu poder en acte·s mostrarà
56   e los meus dits ab los fets provaré.

Tornada

Amor, de vós jo·n sent més que no·n sé,
de què la part pijor me'n romandrà,
e de vós sap lo qui sens vós està.
60   A joc de daus vos acompararé.

that any love for me you might have borne
would also die, and promptly turn to hate.
As for me, when I am driven from this world,
all my pain will be to look on you no more.   36
Oh God, if only there were bounds to love,
for none would be as close to them as I.
Then, between fear and hope no longer torn,
I'd know for sure what love is in your heart.   40

None ever loved to such extremes as I,
save those who for love's sake gave up their lives;
I cannot show the torment of my heart
unless it's by the final proof of death.   44
Good or bad, I am ready for what love
decrees, but Fortune keeps my fate concealed;
love will find me, keeping vigil, gates unbarred,
humbly prepared to do what it commands.   48

The very thing I pray will happen soon
could cost me dear, yet this alone consoles.
When that event most fearful comes to pass,
I ask of God He will not spare my life.   52
For then with their own eyes will people see
the outward signs of all love works in me
–potentiality in act revealed–
and all my words I shall have proved with deeds.   56

Envoi

Love, if I could understand you as I feel!
To me can only fall the loser's share;
no one can know you while he's in your thrall.
How to define you? Let's say a game of dice.   60

LXIV

Lo temps és tal que tot animal brut
requer amor, cascú trobant son par:
lo cervo brau sent en lo bosc bramar,
4   e son fer bram per dolç cant és tengut;
agrons e corbs han melodia tanta
que llur semblant, delitant, enamora.
Lo rossinyol de tal cas s'entrenyora
8   si lo seu cant sa enamorada espanta.

E, doncs, si·m dolc, lo dolre'm és degut
com veig amats menys de poder amar,
e lo grosser per apte veig passar:
12   amor lo fa ésser no conegut.
E d'açò·m ve piadosa complanta
com desamor eixorba ma senyora,
no coneixent lo servent qui l'adora,
16   ne vol pensar qual és sa amor ne quanta.

No com aquell qui son bé ha perdut,
metent a risc si poria guanyar,
he vós amat que·m volguésseu amar:
20   deliberat no só en amor vengut.
Tot nu me trop, vestit de grossa manta;
ma voluntat, amor la té en penyora,
e ço de què mon cor se adolora
24   és com no veu ma fretura que és tanta.

Tornada

Llir entre cards, ab milans caç la ganta
i ab lo branxet la llebre corredora:
assats al món cascuna és vividora.
28   E mon pits flac lo Passi de Rams canta.

LXIV

Now is the time that every brute beast roams
in search of love, and each will find his mate:
the roar of rutting stags fills every wood,
coarse bellow passing for the sweetest trill,   4
herons and crows with melodious warbling
enchant their like, and so secure their love.
How shall the nightingale not weep to see
his song makes the beloved flee in fright?   8

And so, if now I am full of sorrow
it's because I see that those with no idea
of love are loved, and louts become past masters,
for love makes sure that no one finds them out.   12
This is why I make such pitiful complaint:
my lady's blinded by her lack of love,
she quite ignores the servant who adores her
and gives no thought whatever to his love.   16

I have not loved you so that in return
you'd love me too the way a gambler might,
wagering all he had and going for broke:
I did not come to love with gain in mind.   20
One sole coarse blanket hides my shirtless back,
and I have had to pawn my will to love;
but what above all else torments my heart
is that you fail to see my wretchedness.   24

Envoi

Lily among thorns, I hunt storks with kites
and lapdogs send to catch fleet-footed hares:
neither need fear their life runs any risk.
And my faint heart the Passion will intone.   28

LXVIII

No·m PREN AIXÍ com al petit vailet
qui va cercant senyor qui festa·l faça,
tenint-lo cald en lo temps de la glaça
4 e fresc d'estiu com la calor se met,
preant molt poc la valor del senyor
e concebent desalt de sa manera,
veent molt clar que té mala carrera
8 de canviar son estat en major.

Jo son aquell qui en lo temps de tempesta,
quan les més gents festegen prop los focs,
e pusc haver ab ells los propis jocs,
12 vaig sobre neu, descalç, ab nua testa,
servint senyor qui jamés fon vassall
ne·l venc esment de fer mai homenatge;
en tot lleig fet hagué lo cor salvatge;
16 solament diu que bon guardó no·m fall.

Tornada

Plena de seny, lleigs desigs de mi tall.
Herbes no·s fan males en mon ribatge:
sia entés com dins en mon coratge
20 los pensaments no·m devallen avall.

LXVIII

IT'S JUST THE opposite with me as with
that little page who thinks that he dislikes
his master's ways, quite blinded to his worth,
expecting he should keep him snug and warm   4
in frost, and cool throughout the summer months,
and seeks another, pampering, master,
but promptly learns the error he has made:
as good as he once had he'll never find.   8

Such am I: while others give themselves to fun
and I too could make merry round their hearths,
barefoot I labour through the driven snow,
my head uncovered to the raging storm,   12
serving a master who is no man's liege
and to no lord would ever homage pay;
his ruthless heart would scorn no ugly deed;
his only words: that there'll be good reward.   16

Envoi

Beauteous Wisdom, ugly desires all
in me I cut and slash; my field is free
of every noxious weed. By this I mean
my heart will hold no thoughts that drag me down.   20

LXXX

Tot llaurador és pagat del jornal,
e l'advocat qui perd lo guanyat plet.
Jo, per servir amor, romanc desfet
4   de tot quant he, que servir no me'n cal.
He fet senyor del seny a mon voler,
veent amor de mon seny mal servit;
rapaç l'he fet, e Déu a part jaquit.
8   E són setze anys que lo guardó esper!

Tornada

Amor, Amor, poc és vostre poder
per altre hom com jo fer tant amar.
Anau, anau vostres armes provar
12   en contra aquell qui vostre no vol ser!

LXXX

No LABOURER will be denied his pay,
lawyers can lose the case but have their fee;
I have served love long, but am ruined now;
all my service has proved to be in vain.   4
Since reason refused to do as love bids,
as master over it I've set desire,
made it its thrall, and gave no thought to God.
Sixteen years, and still no hint of reward!   8

Envoi

Oh love, my master, do you really think
that you could make another love like me?
Be off, take up your arms, and try your strength
on one who does not want to be your serf!   12

LXXXI

Així com cell qui·s veu prop de la mort,
corrent mal temps, perillant en la mar,
e veu lo lloc on se pot restaurar,
4   e no hi ateny per sa malvada sort,
ne pren a me qui vaig afanys passant
e veig a vós bastant mos mals delir.
Desesperat de mos desigs complir,
8   iré pel món vostre ergull recitant.

LXXXI

LIKE ONE IN peril on the storm-tossed sea
who knows that death awaits him close at hand,
and meanwhile sees the safety of the shore
–in vain, for adverse fate soon sends him down–   4
so must I suffer all the pain of love
which you could cure, yet watch you from afar.
Bereft of hope, desires all unfulfilled,
the world I'll wander, singing of your pride.   8

LXXXIII

Sí co·l malalt qui llong temps ha que jau
e vol un jorn esforçar-se llevar,
e sa virtut no li pot molt aidar,
4   ans, llevat dret, sobtament plegat cau:
ne pren a mi que m'esforç contra amor
e vull seguir tot ço que mon seny vol.
Complir no ho pusc perquè la força·m tol
8   un mal extrem atraçat per amor.

LXXXIII

LIKE THE INVALID long to bed confined
who one day tries to struggle to his feet,
but finds he simply does not have the strength,
and at the first step crumples to the ground,   4
so with me, as I struggle against love
and strive to act as reason has ordained,
my strength will always fail me while love plies
its special pain, invented just for me.   8

POEMS OF PRAISE AND BLAME

XXIII

Lleixant a part l'estil dels trobadors
qui, per escalf, traspassen veritat,
e sostraent mon voler afectat
4   perquè no·m torb, diré·l que trob en vós.
Tot mon parlar als qui no us hauran vista
res no valrà, car fe no hi donaran,
e los veents que dins vós no veuran,
8   en creure a mi, llur arma serà trista.

L'ull de l'hom pec no ha tan fosca vista
que vostre cos no jutge per gentil;
no·l coneix tal com lo qui és subtil;
12   hoc la color, mas no sap de la llista.
Quant és del cos menys de participar
ab l'esperit, coneix bé lo grosser:
vostra color i el tall pot bé saber,
16   mas ja del gest no porà bé parlar.

Tots som grossers en poder explicar
ço que mereix un bell cos e honest;
jóvens gentils, bons, sabents, l'han request
20   e, famejants, los cové endurar.
Lo vostre seny fa ço que altre no basta,
que sap regir la molta subtilea.
En fer tot bé, s'adorm en vós perea.
24   Verge no sou perquè Déu ne volc casta.

Sol per a vós bastà la bona pasta
que Déu retenc per fer singulars dones.
Fetes n'ha assats, molt sàvies e bones,
28   mas compliment dona Teresa·l tasta,
havent en si tan gran coneiximent
que res no·l fall que tota no·s conega.
A l'hom devot sa bellesa encega;
32   past d'entenents és son enteniment.

XXIII

I DON'T NEED to write like the troubadours,
all so inflamed that truth's soon left behind;
and, fervent though it is, I'll quell desire
and only then say what I find in you.   4
On those who have not seen you for themselves,
my words are lost: just lies, they all will say;
but those who've seen you–yet just the outer self–
will know that I speak true: their hearts will sink.   8

The very dimmest wits could never miss
the marks your person bears of noble blood;
discerning eyes will soon perceive much more;
a fool views cloth by colour, quality's lost.   12
Ignorant men know all about the body,
except where spirit also has its part.
Much they can say of your cut and hue;
but all before your beauty are struck dumb.   16

Yet everyone's a dolt to find the words
to paint the beauty of your virtuous form.
Nobles, young and good and wise, have pleaded:
ever will they hunger; so must it be.   20
Equal to yours there is no other mind;
the subtlest concepts lie within its grasp;
sloth must sleep as your goodness does it work.
Not virgin, but mother, such was God's will.   24

You He formed from the substance He saves
for making special women of great worth;
He created many such, most wise and good,
yet perfect none but Lady Teresa,   28
others in her wisdom far excelling;
nothing lies beyond the reach of her wit;
devoutest gaze is by her beauty stunned;
her mind is bread to feed enlightened minds.   32

Venecians no han lo regiment
tan pacific com vostre seny regeix
subtilitats que l'entendre us nodreix
36   e del cos bell sens colpa·l moviment.
Tan gran delit tot hom entenent ha
e ocupat se troba en vós entendre,
que lo desig del cos no·s pot estendre
40   a lleig voler, ans com a mort està.

Tornada

Llir entre cards, lo meu poder no fa
tant que pogués fer corona invisible.
Meriu-la vós, car la qui és visible
44   no·s deu posar lla on miracle està.

Venice the Most Serene can only envy
your mind's calm governance of subtlest thoughts,
sole nourishment of your understanding,
and the guiltless movements of your lovely form.   36
Enlightened men set all their wits to grasp
your thoughts, reaping from them such rare delight
that bodily desire can never stir,
and all base urges slumber undisturbed.   40

                    Envoi

Lily among thorns, would I had the power
to place an unseen crown upon your head.
No other crown will do: the kind that's seen
must ill befit a living miracle.   44

XLII

Vós qui sabeu de la tortra·l costum,
e si no ho feu, plàcia'l-vos oir:
quan mort li tol son par, se vol jaquir
4   d'obres d'amor, ne beu aigua de flum,
ans en los clots ensutza primer l'aigua,
ne·s posa mai en verd arbre fullat.
Mas contra açò és vostra qualitat,
8   per gran desig no cast que en vós se raiga.

E no cuideu, dona, que bé us escaiga
que, pus hagués tastat la carn gentil,
a mercader lliuràs vostre cos vil,
12   e son dret nom En Joan me pens caiga.
E si voleu que us ne don coneixença,
sa faç és gran e la vista molt llosca;
sos fonaments són de llagost o mosca.
16   Cert no mereix draps vendre de Florença.

E coneixent la vostra gran fallença,
volgué's muntar, en amar, cavaller.
E sabent ell tot vostre fet en ver
20   en vós amar se tengra a consciença,
sabent molt clar la sutzeada vida,
prenent public les pagues del pecat.
Vostre cos lleig per drap és baratat;
24   vostre servir és bo sol per a dida.

E no cuideu filla us hagués jaquida,
vós alletant aquella ab vostra llet,
car vostre cos és de verí replet,
28   e mostren-ho vostres pèls fora mida;
car si us jaquiu vostra barba criada
e la us toleu, puis ab los pèls dels braços
poran-se fer avantajosos llaços,
32   prenints perdius, tortra, o cogullada.

XLII

YOU MUST HAVE heard about the turtle-dove;
well, if you haven't, listen to the tale.
When death takes her mate, she bids love farewell,
and ceases to drink from the running stream,   4
fouling the puddles where she slakes her thirst,
and never perches on the green-leafed tree.
A different story are you and your ways:
in you a monstrous lust has taken root.   8

Don't think, madam, that any good could come
of giving to a merchant your foul corpse,
after it had savoured some noble flesh!
Dick's his name, as well could be expected.   12
You know, I am sure, the fellow I mean:
the big-faced one who has that ghastly squint,
a pair of legs like a fly or locust.
A fine one to be selling cloth from Florence!   16

Because he knew your worse defects, he thought
by mounting you he'd amount to a knight.
But if he learnt the truth about your life,
just how sordid it is and foul, of how   20
you've paid in public the price of your sins,
he'd soon repent of giving you his love.
You've sold your body for a piece of cloth,
and now wet-nursing can be your only use!   24

Don't think he's put a baby girl in you
that with your milk you'll be able to feed,
for your whole body is swollen with pus:
those monstrous hairs upon it say it all;   28
why, if you were to let your beard grow long,
to weave it with the hair upon your arms,
fine hunting-snares they'd make, partridges
to catch, or crested lapwings –or turtle-doves.   32

Quan oireu «Alcavota provada!»,
responeu tost, que per vós ho diran.
E puis per nom propi vos cridaran,
36   ja no us mostreu en l'oir empatxada,
enterrogant, «Amics, ¿e què voleu?
¿En dret d'amor voleu res que fer pusca?
Tracte semblant jamés me trobà cusca.
40   Presta seré a quant demanareu».

Tornada

Tots los qui trop acunçament volreu
en fets d'amor, emprau Na Monboí.
Ella us farà tot lo que féu a mi.
44   No·s pot saber l'endreç que hi trobareu!

'Hey, you, old whore-monger!', people will shout.
Now, don't be bashful, for it's you they'll mean.
You'll know, because they'll call you by your name;
it will do no good pretending that you're deaf; 36
just ask them: 'So, what will it be, my dears?
If it's to do with love, rely on me.
Tell me your desires, and I'll straight to it.
I'll soon get you everything you're after!' 40

Envoi

If any of you needs help in matters
of love, then give Na Monboí a try.
She'll do for you just as she did for me.
You'll all soon see what a lift she'll give you! 44

PHILOSOPHICAL POEMS

XXXII

L'HOME PEL MÓN no munta en gran valer
sens haver béns, bondat, llinatge gran;
mas la del mig val més que lo restan,
e no val molt sens les altres haver.
Per ella·s fan les dues molt prear,
car poder val tant com és ministrat,
llinatge val aitant com és honrat;
la valor d'hom ho fa tot graduar.

Mas no serà l'hom sabent de sonar
si en algun temps no sonà esturment,
car per voler sonar lo nom no·s pren
mas, l'esturment sonant, bé acordar.
Tot enaixí, aquell qui dins si val,
pobre de béns e d'avilat llinatge,
no té·ls arreus per mostrar gran coratge
en la virtut que·s nomena moral.

Són e seran molts d'un altre cabal,
havent molts béns e d'alta sang favor
e, valent poc, han la part no mellor
car, sens l'hom bo, quant pot haver és mal.
E moltes veus ha la colpa natura,
car farà bo tal que valer no sap;
negun saber no pot viure en llur cap;
sens colpa llur, de valer han fretura.

Entre·ls extrems al mig virtut atura,
molt greu d'obrar i entre pocs conegut.
Per ell saber no és hom per bo tengut,
mas fets obrant forans dins tal mesura:
aitant és llarg l'hom menys de fer llarguesa
com és escàs si no fall en despendre.
Vicis, virtuts, per actes s'han a pendre;
aprés lo fet és llur potença apresa.

XXXII

GREAT WORTH CAN no man in this world achieve
without possessions, goodness, and high birth;
of these the middle one's what matters most,
yet without the others for little counts.   4
Through it these two are held in high esteem,
for power, to be good, must be used well,
while lineage the honour paid must win;
the man's worth is the measure of it all.   8

But call no man musician until he's learned
to draw true music from an instrument;
wanting to play is not enough to earn
that name, but really to play it, and in tune.   12
Of the man with inner worth the same is true:
poor in worldly goods, and humble of birth,
he lacks the means with which to show his zeal,
practising what men call moral virtue.   16

Others there are many, and will always be,
blessed by high birth and riches, who yet lack
what's most important, for unless the man
is good, of no use will any of these be.   20
And often Nature is at fault, since it will
endow with goodness men without the wit
to use it, to wisdom ever strangers;
true worth eludes them, for no fault of theirs.   24

Virtue shuns extremes and in the mid place lies,
hardest of goals for men, and known to few.
To know this mean will yet not make you good,
but only acts performed accordingly: 28
no man's generous who never shows largesse,
no more than mean if he is always spending.
Only actions show our virtues or our vice,
only through act the potential is known.   32

No·s conquerran virtuts per gran aptesa
ne les hauran poetes per llur art.
Han-les aquells metents vicis a part,
36   obrant virtut per amor de bonesa,
res no dubtant viciosa vergonya,
mas solament amant virtuós preu.
E l'home pec en aquest banc no seu,
40   e qui n'és lluny lo gran delit se llonya.

Tornada

Llir entre cards, tostemps faré ma ponya
que la dolor jamés de mi·s partesca;
e no pensau que mon cas enferesca,
44   car major dan mereix ma gran vergonya.

Cleverness provides no path to virtue,
and poets cannot have it through their art;
only those who set their sinful ways aside,
for good's own sake performing virtuous acts,   36
free of sin and by its shame untroubled,
loving nothing more than virtuous esteem.
There's no room on that bench for brutish men,
but only there the highest good is found.   40

Envoi

Lily among thorns, inseparable
from me will pain for ever be in all I do;
trust me, this is no exaggeration:
even worse does my shameful guilt deserve.   44

LXXXII

Quan plau a Déu que la fusta peresca,
en segur port romp àncores i ormeig,
e de poc mal a molt hom morir veig:
null hom és cert d'algun fet com fenesca.
L'home sabent no té pus avantatge
sinó que·l pec sol menys fets avenir.
L'experiment i els juís veig fallir;
fortuna i cas los torben llur usatge.

LXXXII

When it is God's will that the ship go down,
no port is safe: rigging, anchors, all will break;
and often some small ailment leads to death:
none can foresee how anything will end.   4
The wise man's placed no better than the fool,
save that his guesses are more well informed.
Experience and judgement always fail,
duped by Fortune and by what comes to pass.   8

POEMS ON GRIEF

XCII

AQUELLES MANS que jamés perdonaren
han ja romput lo fil tenint la vida
de vós, qui sou de aquest món eixida
segons los fats en secret ordenaren.
Tot quant jo veig e sent dolor me torna,
dant-me record de vós, qui tant amava.
E en ma dolor, si prim e bé·s cercava,
se trobarà que delit s'hi contorna;
doncs durarà, puis té qui la sostinga,
car sens delit dolor crei no·s retinga.

En cor gentil amor per mort no passa,
mas en aquell que per lo vici·s tira.
La quantitat d'amor durar no mira;
la qualitat d'amor bona no·s llassa.
Quan l'ull no veu e lo toc no·s pratica,
mor lo voler, que tot per ells se guanya;
qui en tal punt és, dolor sent molt estranya,
mas dura poc: l'expert ho testifica.
Amor honest los sants amants fa colre;
d'aquest vos am, e mort no·l me pot tolre.

Tots los volers que en mi confusos eren
se mostren clar per llur obra forana:
ma carn se dol car sa natura ho mana,
perquè en la mort sos delits se perderen;
en sa dolor ma arma és embolcada,
de què llur plor e plant per null temps callen.
En tal dolor tots los conhorts me fallen,
com sens tornar la que am és anada.
Mas l'altra amor, de amistança pura,
aprés sa mort sa força gran li dura.

XCII

THOSE RUTHLESS hands no mortal ever spared
have cut the thread to which your life was bound,
and you have now departed from this world
just as the Fates had secretly ordained.
There's pain in everything I see and feel,   5
since all is full of you, so dearly loved.
And yet, a close inspection of my pain
would show that there is pleasure mingled there
–and so must last, sustained by this delight;
without it, grief I doubt could long endure.   10

In noble hearts love does not end with death,
only in those which are disposed to vice;
quantity does not concern them, how long
love lasts; of good love the quality endures;
when eye does not see and hand cannot touch,   15
desire fails: through these only can it thrive;
this brings a strange but short-lived form of pain,
as all those who have felt it will confirm.
Virtuous love is worshipped by the saints;
this love I bear you, beyond the reach of death.   20

All the desires that once were mixed in me
through their effects can now be told apart;
my flesh grieves just as its nature decrees,
for death has stripped it clean of all delight;
in the body's pain the soul is enmeshed,   25
so the weeping and wailing has no end.
And in such pain, all comfort lets me down,
for now she has gone, never to return.
But such is the power of that other love,
of friendship pure, it lasts beyond her death.   30

Aquesta amor, si los pecs no la creen,
és ver senyal del bé que en ella habita.
Aquesta és qui sens dolor delita,
i els cecs volers de prop aquesta·s veen.
35   Lo voler cec del tot ella il·lumena,
mas no en tant que lleve·l cataracte.
E si posqués fer sens empatx son acte,
no fóra al món ull ab gota serena;
mas és així com la poca triaga:
40   que molt verí sa virtut li apaga.

Aquell voler que en ma carn sola·s causa,
si no és mort, no tardarà que muira.
L'altre, per qui dol continu m'abuira,
si·m defalleix, no serà sens gran causa:
45   ell pot ser dit voler concupiscible,
e sol durar, puis molt de l'arma toca;
mas fall per temps, car virtut no invoca
e d'un costat és apetit sensible.
Aquests volers l'amor honesta·m torben
50   perquè entre mal e bé mes penses orben.

D'arma e cos és compost l'hom, contraris,
per què·l voler e l'apetit contrasten.
Tot quant aquests de llur natura tasten
és saborós e vitals lletovaris.
55   Altre voler que en mig d'aquests camina
és atrobat que no té via certa:
cuida haver port en la plaja deserta
e lo verí li sembla medecina.
Aquest voler ab arma i cos conversa;
60   naix d'ells, e fa la obra d'ells diversa.

Tres són les parts vers on mos volers pugen
e per semblant vénen per tres maneres.
Entre si han contràries carreres,
delits portants e d'altres que m'enugen:
65   quan los delits del cos la pensa·m mostra,
jo sent dolor car són perduts sens cobre.
Altra dolor sent que·m vist tot e·m cobre
com pens que mort ha tolta l'amor nostra.
L'altre voler raó i natura funden,
70   que sens dolor molts delits ne abunden.

Though fools may scoff, the presence of such love
is one sure sign that in it goodness dwells.
This kind of love delights and brings no pain;
other, blind, desires are never far away,
but this love to their eyes restores the light,   35
even if the cataract it can't remove.
If unhindered it could perform its work,
never would still drop cloud a single eye.
But use antidotes in too small a dose,
and poison soon will wipe out their effect.   40

That desire which springs from flesh alone,
if not already dead, will perish soon.
And why should not that other one die too,
that feeds me with its endless draughts of pain?
Concupiscent desire we may call it;   45
the souls's part is great, and so it lingers,
but fades with time, discarding virtue's aid;
sensitive appetite's its other side.
Virtuous love is thwarted by these two,
exalting evil, blinding me to good.   50

Body and soul make man, but they're at war;
hence comes the clash of appetite with will.
When each feeds as its nature would dictate,
their bread's the sweetest balm, infusing life.
But there's one more desire, and this one treads   55
uncertain paths between the other two;
it sees a harbour where there's open beach,
and uses poison for a medicine.
It speaks with body and with soul, and springs
from both, performs the various work of each.   60

Separately, towards three places, strives
each of my desires, and by them is formed.
Each strikes its path, they go in diverse ways,
that bring their own delights, but torments too.
Pain comes with memories of fleshly joy,   65
for this irrecoverably is lost.
Another kind of suffering grips me too
–to think that from us death has stolen love.
Reason and nature form the third desire,
where pleasures thrive, and pain can have no part.   70

Lo lloc on jau la dolor gran que passe
no és del tot fora de mes natures,
ne del tot és fora de llurs clausures;
lo moviment creu que per elles passe.
75   Aquell voler que en mi no troba terme
és lo mijà per on dolor m'agreuja.
L'extrem d'aquest fora natura alleuja,
fort e punyent mas encansable verme;
opinió falsa per tots és dita,
80   que fora nós e dintre nós habita.

D'aquesta amor les demés gents tremolen;
aquesta és sentida i no sabuda:
poques gents han sa causa coneguda.
Delits, dolors, per ella venir solen:
85   lo cos per si lo seu delit desija,
l'arma enaprés lo sent e vol atényer
lo propi seu, al qual no·s pot empényer,
car tot és fals, d'on ella se fastija.
D'aquests contrasts aquesta amor escapa,
90   que veritat no ateny ab sa capa.

Tant és unit lo cos ab la nostra arma
que acte en l'hom no pot ser dit bé simple;
algú no és vers l'altre humil e simple;
contrast se fan, l'u contra l'altre s'arma.
95   Mas és tan poc lo contrast a sa hora
que en fets del cos l'arma no fa gran nosa;
i en contemplant, així l'arma reposa
que, bé représ, lo cos d'açò no plora.
Aquesta pau en mi no és molt llonga,
100   per què dolor més que·l delit s'allonga.

Dolor jo sent, e sembla a mi extrema;
no só en punt de voler consell rebre,
e de negun remei me vull percebre,
ans de tristor he presa ja ma tema.
105   Si·m trop en punt que dolor no m'acorde,
ja tinc senyal ab què a dolor torne:
record sos fets d'amor e allens borne;
d'ací escapant, ab oci no·m concorde:
son esperit sens lo cos jo contemple;
110   tant delit sent com l'hom devot al temple.

Where does this heavy pain I feel reside?
Outside human nature it does not lie,
nor is it so constrained; it moves, I think,
beyond and yet within our human bounds.
That desire which finds no end in me   75
becomes the means by which this pain afflicts;
outside our nature its own end must seek,
a strong and fierce and ever tireless worm.
The common view is wrong: desire like this
dwells in the body, but beyond it yearns.   80

Most people tremble with this kind of love;
many have felt it, but none understood,
and where it comes from few have ever learned.
Both pleasure and pain it brings us: the body
desires pleasure of its own kind, then this   85
spreads to the soul, which strives to find
its own delight, but fails, since the pleasure
felt is false; the soul is left frustrated.
Caught amidst such strife, this love soon leaves us,
for truth beneath its cloak cannot be hid.   90

So closely twined with body is the soul
that simple can be deemed no human act;
humble or docile will neither be; each,
defiant, against the other takes up arms.
Yet so weakly confronted is the body   95
by the soul, it acts quite unimpeded;
while the soul is stilled in contemplation,
the body's free to savour its own good.
In me this peace, which should endure, is short,
since grief all forms of pleasure will outlast.   100

I grieve, and I would say my grief's extreme;
my condition such that I shun all advice,
and I refuse to hear of remedies;
sadness pervades my every thought and deed.
If ever my pain I start to forget,   105
there's one sure way that I can bring it back:
I think of her deeds of love, and pain takes flight.
Thus restored, my thoughts are never idle:
I contemplate her spirit, not the flesh;
the devout man in church feels nothing less.   110

De pietat de sa mort ve que·m dolga,
e só forçat que mon mal haja plànyer.
Tant he perdut que bé no·m pot atànyer;
Fortuna ja no té què pus me tolga.
115   Quan imagín les voluntats unides
i el conversar, separats per a sempre,
pensar no pusc ma dolor haja tempre:
mes passions no trop gens aflaquides,
e si per temps elles passar havien,
120   vengut és temps que començar devien.

Mes voluntats mos pensaments aporten
avall i amunt, sí com los núvols l'aire:
adés me dolc, puis dolor no sent gaire,
e sent dolors que ab si dolors comporten.
125   Quan pens que·ls morts de res dels vius no pensen,
e les dolors que pas sens grat se perden,
mos sentiments han mal, e no s'esperden
tant que d'amor e dolor se defensen.
E pas dolor que en la d'infern s'acosta
130   com en est món no la'm veuré de costa.

En altre món a mi par que jo sia
i els propis fets estranys a mi aparen,
semblant d'aquells que mos juís lloaren.
Lo fals par ver, la veritat falsia:
135   los meus juís la dolor los ofega.
Lo lloc no hi és on primer habitaven;
si és, no tal com ans del cas estaven:
alterat és; la mort ja se'm fa brega,
tal e tan fort que, altre matant, mi mata.
140   No sé com és que lo cor no m'esclata.

Alguns han dit que la mort és amarga:
poden-ho dir los qui la sabor senten
o de per si, o com per altre tenten
sa fort dolor, que entre totes és llarga.
145   Per mi no tem; per altre l'he temuda.
Puis fon cruel, ja pietat no m'haja:
qui en terra jau no tem pus avall caja;
en l'esperat ma esperança és perduda.
Oh partiment dolorós, perdurable,
150   fent en dolor mi comparat diable!

My pity for her death's the cause of grief
and I cannot but bewail what I have lost,
so great, that good I'll never know again;
I've nothing else that Fortune could remove.
When I think that our wills combined would live   115
as one, and must for ever be apart,
there's nothing I believe could ease my pain:
my suffering shows no sign it will abate,
and if it's true with time it must subside,
the hour's long past when this should have begun.   120

Up and down by desires my thoughts are pushed
that shift and change like clouds before the wind;
now I grieve, now scarce anything I feel,
then pain comes back, and in its wake more pain.
When I think the dead for us who live   125
can have no thought, that my suffering's all
in vain, then sentiment begins to fade,
but not so much it keeps out love and pain.
To know I'll see her nevermore beside me
brings torment that can be no less than Hell's.   130

This is like living in a different world:
none of my actions seems to be my own,
yet strangely like what I had thought to do.
All that's false seems true, and truth seems falsehood,
my sense of what is true quite drowned in pain;   135
good judgement no longer in me resides;
or, if it does, then not as previously;
utterly it's changed: such war death wages
that, killing another, it kills me too.
Why yet my heart's not burst I can't explain.   140

Some have called death bitter; but only those
can rightly speak of it who for themselves
know its taste, or else have felt its fierce pain
–longest pain of all– because of someone else.
My fear's not for myself, but another.   145
Since death was cruel, its pity's of no use:
once a man's cast down, he can no further fall;
in all I hoped for, I have lost all hope.
Oh painful parting without end, bringing
torments whose like none but the Devil knows.   150

No preu los béns que jo sols posseesca
car plaent res home sol no pratica.
La mort no tem que lo món damnifica
sinó que tem que·l cel me defallesca.
155 Tot cas jo mir ab una egual cara;
res no·m fa trist, e ja molt menys alegre;
no és color dessobre blanc o negre;
vers mi no hi ha cosa escura ne clara.
Tot quant amor e por me pogren noure
160 finí lo jorn que li viu los ulls cloure.

Segons lo cas, ma dolor no és tanta
com se requer per un mortal damnatge;
sobre tots mals la mort porta avantatge;
jo l'he sentit, e de present m'espanta.
165 Segons l'amor, del dan no port gran signe;
e volgra jo que en lo món fos notable,
dient cascú: «Veus l'home pus amable»,
e que plangués cascú mon fat maligne.
Aquell voler causat per cosa honesta,
170 mentre seré, serà mostrant gran gesta.

Tan comun cas, ¿per què tan extrem sembla
al qui per sort la mort en tant lo plaga?
¿Per què en tal cas la raó d'hom s'amaga
e passió tota sa força assembla?
175 Déu, piadós e just, cruel se mostra,
tant és en nós torbada coneixença;
fluixant dolor, primer plega creença,
mas ferm saber no és en potença nostra.
Als que la mort tol la muller aimia
180 sabran jutjar part de la dolor mia.

Tot ver amic a son ver amic ama
de tal amor que mort no la menyscaba;
ans és fornal que apura l'or i acaba,
lleixant-lo fi, e l'àls en fum derrama.
185 D'aquesta amor am aquella que és morta
e tement am tot quant és de aquella.
L'esperit viu; doncs, ¿quina maravella
que am aquell e res tant no·m conforta?
Membra'm la mort e torn en ma congoixa,
190 e quan hi só, dolor pas com me floixa.

I scorn the good I could enjoy alone:
alone, no man can ever find delight.
I fear no harm from death, not in this world;
rather, I fear that Heaven will fail me.
The same face I show, whatever comes my way;   155
nothing makes me sad, and much less content;
for me things are coloured neither black nor white,
and neither dark nor brightness can I find.
All the hurt that love and fear could do me
ceased the day that she for ever closed her eyes.   160

Painful in extreme is this event, and yet
not great enough to cause a mortal wound;
but death will outdo evil of all kinds:
I have felt it; still with dread it fills me.
Judged as a lover, I bear no mark of pain,   165
yet I would have men point me out and say,
'He's the world's one true and perfect lover',
and have them all bewail my evil fate.
That desire which in virtue is founded,
while my life may last, will achieve great deeds.   170

Why does an event as common as death
seem so severe to whomever it wounds?
Why at such times does man's reason retreat
and the passions muster all their power?
God, compassionate, just, seems cruel to us,   175
our understanding so greatly is perplexed;
the pain abates, and faith at once returns,
but firm understanding lies beyond our power.
He has some inkling of my pain whom death
has robbed of she who was his wife-beloved.   180

Every true friend his own true friend will love
with such firm love as cannot shrink with death;
for death's the crucible where gold's refined,
perfected into purity, all dross
sent off in smoke; such is my love for her,   185
and I fear for her and all that's hers I love.
Her spirit lives. So is it any wonder
that spirit is my love and consolation?
I think of her death, and torment returns,
but the suffering's worse if the pain relents.   190

Accident és amor, e no substança,
e per sos fets se dóna a nós conéixer;
quant és ne qual, ell se dóna a paréixer;
segons d'on part, així sa força llança.
195   Sí com lo vent, segons les encontrades
on és passat, de si cald o fred gita,
així amor dolor da o delita
segons lo for del lloc on ha llançades
fondes raïls: o sus cara de terra,
200   o sobre fang, o sus molt aspra serra.

Amor en l'hom dos llocs disposts atroba,
car hom és dit per ses dues natures;
lo cos per si vol semblant de sutzures;
l'arma per si d'un blanc net vol sa roba;
205   d'ells aünits surt amor d'algun acte
que no·s diu bé qual d'ells més part hi faça.
Cascú per si algun delit acaça
i, aquell atés, l'altre·n porta caractc.
E veus la mort que llur voler termena;
210   lo bo no pot: no basta que l'ofena.

Morint lo cos, a son amant no·l resta
sinó dolor per lo record del plaure;
fallint aquell, no tarda amor en caure:
fallint lo sant, defall la sua festa.
215   Alguns delits que en l'arma pel cos vénen
són los composts que·ls amadors turmenten,
e cascú d'ells tanta i qual dolor senten
segons del cos o de l'arma part prenen;
e mort l'amat, amor és duradora
220   tant quant lo mort del viu té gran penyora.

Ço que en passat embolt e confús era
és departit; lo gra no és ab la palla:
experiment altre no·m pens hi valla:
per la mort és oberta la carrera.
225   Ma carn no sent; doncs, no·s pot fer que ame,
car ja no és ço que sentir li feia.
Si voler tinc, pec és lo qui no creia
que l'esperit de pura amor s'enflame,
cobejant molt que Déu s'arma s'emporte.
230   Açò dubtant, que jo pena reporte.

Love's defined as accident, not substance;
only by its actions can we know it;
by these its nature and strength are revealed,
which are only as its origins allow.
Just as the wind blows hot or cold after   195
it's swept through lands that are cold or hot,
so pleasure comes from love, or there is pain,
in accordance with the place where its roots
have deepest sunk: into the shallow soil,
or into mud, or on the rugged tor.   200

Love finds in man two parts disposed to love,
for his dual nature is what makes him man;
the body for itself wants only filth,
but the soul would have its robes of purest white;
from their union certain deeds of love will spring,   205
such that it's hard to tell which takes the lead.
Each for itself seeks pleasure in some form,
and some mark of it upon the other leaves.
Along comes death and kills their shared delight;
pure desire's untouched; death has there no right.   210

Once the body's dead, its lover is left
with grievous memories of pleasure lost;
the memory fades, and soon love starts to wane:
the feast-day's dropped when the saint is not revered.
Some of the soul's delights the body bears   215
as compound pleasures; these torment lovers,
and such and so strong will they feel this pain
just as much as body or soul holds sway.
Once the loved one's dead, love will last while she
yet holds the living to their binding pledge.   220

What in the past was tangled and confused
is lost; the chaff is winnowed from the grain;
but for grief, this I think could not have been:
the road has been opened by death itself.
Since my flesh feels nothing, it cannot love,   225
now the one cause of all it felt is dead.
Desire lingers, but none should crassly doubt
that with pure love my spirit is inflamed,
my deepest wish her spirit God should take.
My soul be damned if ever I should doubt.   230

Si en nostra amor pens ésser fi venguda,
e d'ella perd esperança de veure,
sinó que tost vinc en açò descreure,
l'arma en lo cos no fóra retenguda.
235   Si bé los morts en lo món no retornen,
ans d'ésser mort noves sabré d'aquella.
Estat és ja; doncs, no és gran maravella,
açò esperant, mos sentiments sojornen.
E si cert fos que entre los sants fos mesa,
240   no volgra jo que de mort fos defesa.

Oh Déu, mercé! Mas, no sé de què·t pregue,
sinó que mi en lo seu lloc aculles.
No·m tardes molt que dellà mi no vulles
puis l'esperit on és lo seu aplegue.
245   E lo meu cos, ans que la vida fine,
sobre lo seu abraçat vull que jaga.
Ferí'ls amor de no curable plaga,
separà'ls mort: dret és que ella·ls veïne.
Lo jorn del Jui, quan pendrem carn e ossos,
250   mescladament partirem nostres cossos.

Whenever I think our love has reached its end
and I lose hope of seeing her again,
I must at once such thoughts dispel, or else
my soul no longer could in body dwell.
Even though the dead can never return,   235
before I die I shall have news of her.
She has gone, but while I live in hope of news,
is it so strange my feelings should not change?
If I could be sure she with the blessed dwells,
I would not wish that she were still alive.   240

Oh Lord have mercy! But I scarcely know
what now I ask: to be with her, that's all.
Do not exclude me from that place too long;
my spirit longs for hers, to be where she is.
As for my body, before I leave this life,   245
upon hers let it lie in close embrace.
The wound love dealt them both can never heal;
but death can unite them, that drove apart.
Come Judgement Day, we shall return to flesh,
and each to each shall we our bodies share.   250

XCIII

¿Qui serà aquell del món superior
que veritat de vós a mi recont?
¿E qui sap dir on serà aquell afront
que nós haurem, portant goig o dolor?
Los llocs seran mostrants lo bé o mal
segons en ells mal o bé·s contendrà;
e si nós dos un lloc no ocuparà,
lo partiment serà perpetual.

L'esguard que jo de vós he no és egual,
així divers és o contrariant:
les penes grans d'infern jo só dubtant
(tot quant n'he llest a dolorir me val),
e puis ve temps que us imagín al món
haver ab mi verdadera amistat.
Aquell delit que·l món pot haver dat
fort cor és ops a membrar lo que fon.

Lo dolorós e miserable don,
estrany e molt, mas prestament perdut,
és tot ço quant en lo món he haüt.
La mort l'ha tolt e portat no sé on;
ma fort dolor no basta fer voler
que l'amistat fos estada no res,
ans só content d'aquella que fos més,
si bé tristor per aquella sofer.

¿On és aquell qui no espera plaer
e no ha esguard a bona o mala fi?
Mira lo món; veu-se jove, i mesquí
com ja no és on ferme son voler.
Dreça sos ulls envers la part del cel
e diu a Déu, ab gest no sats humil,
paraules tals que puis se'n té per vil;
mas l'hom irat davant raó té vel.

XCIII

Is THERE NO spirit from the higher world
can still my fears about what fate is yours?
If only I knew where next we shall meet,
and if there will be cause for joy or pain.   4
Each place will speak of evil or of good,
fitting the good or evil it contains,
but if one place is not to hold us both,
then we must spend eternity apart.   8

Never the same is the picture I have
of you, its shapes so varied or conflicting;
of Hell's dreadful torments I live in fear
(all I've read of them fills me with terror),   12
I think then of how in this world you were,
the true and loving friendship which was ours:
the stoutest heart would shrink if it recalled
the wordly pleasure that we two enjoyed.   16

This was the one boon –wretched as it is,
most strange, and full of pain, and lost too soon–
that ever I wrung from this world of men.
Death has taken her, but I don't know where;   20
yet pain like this in no amount could make me
want that our friendship never had begun;
rather, I wish that it had long endured,
for all the sadness that it brings me now.   24

Who ever acts with no thought of pleasure,
of whether things will turn out well or ill?
He looks about him: he's still in his youth,
but wretched, with nowhere to fix his love.   28
Heavenwards he lifts his eyes, humility
forgotten, and to God he speaks such words
as later will quite fill him with remorse;
but over man's reason anger draws a veil.   32

Oh Déu! ¿Per què no romp l'amarga fel
aquell qui veu a son amic perir?
Quant més pus vol tan dolça mort sofrir,
36 gran sabor ha, pus se pren per tal zel.
Tu, pietat, ¿com dorms en aquell cas,
que·l cor de carn fer esclatar no saps?
No tens poder, que tal fet no acabs.
40 ¿Qual tan cruel que en tal cas no·t lloàs?

Arquer no sé que tres ocells plagàs
ab un sol colp, que no fos ben content,
matant los dos, i el terç en estament
44 que per mig mort o prop de mort portàs.
Mort en un colp los tres béns m'ha ferits;
los dos són morts: l'útil e·l delitós;
e si l'honest perdés del cel recors,
48 sos darrers jorns serien ja finits.

Jo no puc dir que no senta delits
del pensament, pus que perdre no·l vull:
en lo meu mal algun bé s'hi recull,
52 tal que·l plaer present met en oblits.
Pense cascú quant fon ans de sa mort,
que, perdut ell, jo n'avorresc tot bé.
No sé on jau si record no·l sosté,
56 car tots mos senys han perdut llur deport.

Per bé que·ls dits dels savis jo record,
reptant aquells qui allarguen son dol,
e jo sabí que bona raó vol
60 que null remei és dolre's del qui és mort,
e tot quant l'hom per sa voluntat fa
se deu dreçar a alguna bona part,
e que lo dol, si és tolt, ix d'hom tard,
64 car certament en ell delit està,

però, si dol mai raó·l comportà,
aquest serà que jo en present sostenc.
Un tal delit ab sabor agra hi prenc,
68 que en desijar altre bé cor no·m va.

Oh, God! Why does he not burst with bitter gall
who looks on helpless while his dear friend dies?
The more he longs for that sweet death, the more
he relishes the taste of that longing.   36
How is it, pity, you sleep through it all,
and cannot make a heart of mere flesh burst?
Are you so crippled it's beyond your power?
There's none so cruel as would not praise the deed.   40

No archer would be less than well content
to bring down three birds with a single shot,
killing two outright, leaving the other
half alive or drawing its last breath.   44
With a single blow has death in me struck
all three forms of good; two lie dead: the useful,
the pleasurable; and if Heaven's aid
the chaste one lost, then its days too are done.   48

I cannot claim there's no delight for me
in thinking of the past, to which I cling;
in my suffering there's a kind of good
that eclipses any present pleasure.   52
People can imagine how great was that joy
for me to hate, once lost, all other good.
But only in memory must this pleasure survive,
for all my senses now are in disuse.   56

I haven't forgotten the words of the wise
rebuking those who would prolong their grief,
or that reason tells us all our weeping
for one who's dead will not undo our loss,   60
and all that man does of his own free will
should always be directed to some good,
or that when we choose grief's end, it subsides
but slowly, since some pleasure's surely there   64

–while all this I know, if reason ever
grief condoned, now it does so for this loss.
There's a bitter tasting pleasure in my grief;
from every other good I turn away;   68

Riure jamés no·m plac tant com est plor;
l'aigua dels ulls res tan dolç no m'apar.
No prenc enyor si no·m puc delitar:
72   contra la mort me trop esforçat cor.

E si tots temps en continu no plor,
de mon record aquella no·m partesc;
ans vull que dol me lleixque si·l jaquesc,
76   mon sentiment vull que muira si mor.
Puis que delit a ma dolor segueix,
ingrat seré si ella no m'acost.
Tal sentiment de mal e bé compost,
80   temps minva·l mal, e lo bé tots jorns creix.

Un gran delit en ma pensa·s nodreix
quan algun fet sens la mort d'ella pens;
quan me percep, de dolor no·m defens,
84   pensant que mort per tostemps nos parteix.
Aquest delit la pensa·l fa e·l perd:
foc és mon mal, e mon bé sembla fum.
En aquest cas de somni té costum:
88   bé sent durment, e mal quan só despert.

Jo no puc dir que no sia desert
de tot delit, quan morta l·imagín.
De mi mateix m'espant quan jo m'afín
92   pensant sa mort, e·m par que no·n só cert.
Tal mudament he vist en temps tan breu
que·l qui·m volgué voler a mi no pot,
ne sent ne veu, n'entén si·l dic mon vot.
96   E tot és bé, puis és obra de Déu.

Tornada

A tu qui est mare i filla de Déu,
suplique molt, puis Ell no·m vol oir,
que en aquest món sa arma pusca venir,
100   perquè m'avís on és l'estatge seu.

compared with this, the joys of laughter pale;
nothing to me seems sweeter than these tears.
None of those delights I miss that once I had:
with bold heart can I thus stand up to death.   72

Even if not every hour is filled with tears,
she's absent not one moment from my thoughts;
I only shall decide when grief shall end;
save with my death, these feelings shall not die.   76
Since my pain brings this pleasure in its wake,
ungratefully I will not turn my back.
Of these feelings made up of good and bad,
the good thrives and the bad shrinks day by day.   80

Whenever I forget that she is dead,
and think of something that she did, deep joy
fills me; then the truth sets in, and with it pain
to think that death has parted us for ever.   84
My own thoughts make this pleasure, then destroy:
my pain's the fire, the good is only smoke.
It's then my thoughts are like my dreams: asleep,
there's good, but then I wake, and all is pain.   88

I cannot claim to be bereft of joy
even when I'm most conscious she is dead.
My own thoughts frighten me, for I do not
appear to believe it's true; so rapid   92
and so utter is the change that I have seen:
the one who loved me now can love no more,
she neither feels nor sees, nor hears my prayers.
But all is good that is the work of God.   96

Envoi

You who are mother and daughter of God,
you I beseech, since He will not hear me,
only let her spirit come to me here,
and say which is the place where it must dwell.   100

XCIV

PUIS ME TROP SOL en amor, a mi sembla
que en mi tot sol sia costum estranya:
amor se perd entre gents per absença,
4   e per la mort la mia amor no fina;
ans molt més am a vós en mort que en vida,
e jo perdon si algú no·m vol creure:
pocs són aquells qui altres coses creguen
8   sinó semblants d'aquelles que·ls avenen.

Ma dolor fort lo comun córs no serva:
tota dolor lo temps la venç e gasta.
No dic que en tot a tota altra dessemble:
12   en quantitat molt prop d'altres se jutja;
en qualitat ab les altres discorda,
seguint l'amor d'on ella pren sa forma.
Gran part del temps seca dolor me dóna,
16   i algun delit ab altra dolor dolça.

Dins lo cos d'hom les humors se discorden;
de temps en temps llur poder se transmuda;
en un sols jorn regna malenconia,
20   'n aquell mateix còlera, sang, e fleuma:
tot enaixí les passions de l'arma
mudament han, molt divers o contrari,
car en un punt per ella·s fan los actes
24   e prestament és en lo cos la causa.

Així com l'or que de la mena·l traen
està mesclat de altres metalls sútzeus
e, mes al foc, en fum se'n va la lliga,
28   lleixant l'or pur, no podent-se corrompre,
així la mort mon voler gros termena:
aquell fermat en la part contrassemble
d'aquella que la mort al món l'ha tolta,
32   l'honest voler en mi roman sens mescla.

XCIV

Since none is more alone in love, in me
only could it assume a form so strange:
in others absence causes love to wane,
but my love boundless lives beyond your death: 4
more I love in death than ever in life,
and those who don't believe me I forgive:
few will give credit to the things they hear,
except what they've experienced themselves.   8

My deep pain does not take the normal course;
time will usually wear it all away.
I don't claim it's quite unlike all other
kinds of pain, if quantitively measured;   12
but in quality it differs utterly,
due to the form of love from which it springs.
This inflicts mostly pain and pain alone,
but there's a sweet pain too, that brings delight.   16

Within man's body, the humours are at war,
with shifts in power from one hour to the next;
and all in the space of the selfsame day
melancholy, phlegm, choler, blood prevail;   20
so too the passions of the soul are subject
to change, of many and conflicting kinds,
since the soul one moment will prompt an act,
and the body cause another in the next.   24

Just as gold, when it's brought up from the mine,
does not come pure, but mixed with baser ores,
and then incorruptible is made through fire
as the impure alloy dissolves in smoke,   28
so death all bodily desire has killed:
in the carnal part was such desire fixed
of she whom death has stolen from the world;
so purged, alone survives the part that's chaste.   32

Dos volers són que natura segueixen
e cascú d'ells l'hom per natura guien.
Si acte ensems fan, mal o bé atracen
36   segons qual d'ells en l'altre ha domini;
quan la raó l'apetit senyoreja,
és natural de l'hom tota sa obra,
e lo revers sa natura li torba
40   e no ateny la fi que en tots fets cerca.

Quan l'apetit segueix la part de l'arma,
l'home va dret, seguint natura mestra,
(car la major part la menor se tira),
44   e vers la fi que va lo camí troba.
E l'apetit, volent son necessari,
l'home no fall, si no traspassa l'orde;
e si s'estén més que natura dicta,
48   surt-ne voler fals opinionàtic.

Les voluntats que per natura vénen
en certitud e terme són compreses;
l'altre voler passa d'hom les natures:
52   son senyal cert és que no l'enclou terme.
De tots aquests, passions m'atengueren
mescladament: sí com mesclats jaïen.
Mas bé distints són aprés de son obte
56   e separats los sent, quasi visibles.

Molts són al món que mos dits no entengueren,
e ja molts més que d'aquells no sentiren:
¿Qui creure pot que entre amors vicioses
60   voler honest treball per estar simple,
gitant de si maravellós efecte,
estant secret per força dels contraris?
Dolç i agre ensems, llur sabor no és distinta;
64   ella vivint, mos volers aitals foren.

Dolre's del mort ve de amor comuna,
e de açò jo·m sent tot lo damnatge:
fugir les gents quisque sien alegres
68   i haver despit que jamés lo dol fine.

Man's nature is governed by two forces,
and he by both is naturally compelled.
Acting together, good they bring or ill
as dominance to one falls or the other.   36
Whenever reason governs appetite,
reasonable then is every human deed;
the other way round, nature's confounded,
and unattained the goal for which man strives.   40

As long as appetite obeys the soul,
nature is man's master and leads him straight
(for a great mass a smaller will attract),
and he finds the way to where he wants to go.   44
While appetite seeks only what it needs,
then man it will sustain, if kept within
the natural order; this exceeded,
desire both false and fallible takes root.   48

Those desires that from man's nature arise
are bound to the finite and to the known;
that other desire man's nature exceeds:
this we can tell because it knows no bounds.   52
All mixed together I felt the passions
of these desires, and such they always were.
But now she's dead, I can tell them apart,
each separately feel, and almost see.   56

Many have not grasped what my poems mean,
and even more have never heard of them.
Who could believe in midst of sinful love,
that virtuous desire ever could break free,   60
working upon me its wondrous effects,
secretly cheating its enemies' power?
Both sweet and bitter, their taste was all one;
as long as she lived, such was my desire.   64

Grief for the dead springs from the kind of love
common to us all; in me it's done its worst:
I flee from anyone not sad like me,
and loathe the thought my grief could ever end.   68

Tot delit fuig com a cosa enemiga,
car un bé poc entre grans mals dol porta;
e met poder que·m torn dolor en hàbit
72   perquè de goig la sabor jamés taste.

Senyals d'amor que en tal cas hòmens senten
jo trop en mi que sens dolor se prenen.
Si res començ, jo·n corromp lo principi,
76   per què la fi de res mi no contenta;
molt e pus fort, tota amor me da fàstig,
e sembla a mi ser cosa abominable;
si algun delit entre mes dolors mescle,
80   de fet lo perd, e torn a ma congoixa.

Si·l pensament per força a altra part llance,
d'ella acordant, ab gran sospir lo cobre;
en lo començ ab dolor en mi entra;
84   no passa molt que m'és dolor plaïble.
Decrepitud ma natura demostra,
car tota carn a vòmit me provoca.
Grans amadors per llur aimia morta
88   són mi semblants en part; al tot no basten.

Si res jo veig d'ella, dolor me dóna,
e si·n defuig, par que d'ella m'aparte;
los temps e llocs ab lo dit la'm senyalen,
92   segons en ells delits o dolors foren,
e són-ne tals que la'm demostren trista,
altres, e molts, mostrants aquella alegre.
E pas dolor com jamés li fiu greuge,
96   e volgra açò ab la mia sang rembre.

Amor és dat conéixer pels efectes;
sa quantitat no té mesura certa:
gran és, o poc, l'amador segons altre,
100   e poder pren amor segons on entra.
La qualitat és tal com segons guarda,
car de semblants és forçat que s'engendre:
la carn vol carn, l'arma son semblant cerca;
104   d'ells naix fill bort, als engendrants contrari.

I run from all pleasure as from a foe:
amidst great ills the smallest boon brings woe;
I strive to make my life one round of pain
so that I'll never know the taste of joy.   72

Those signs of love that mark the common grief
appear in me in almost painless form.
Everything I do must from the outset fail;
this I ensure, and scotch satisfaction;   76
worse still, any talk of love revolts me,
for love abhorrent seems in every way;
no sooner pleasure with the pain is mixed
than pleasure's lost and anguish will return.   80

When I find I must attend to other things,
one thought of her, and pain and sighs rush back;
and yet, while there's pure pain only to begin,
soon it turns to a pleasurable form.   84
As for an aged and decrepit body,
the very thought of flesh will make me retch.
In my grief I have no match, save a few
great lovers –and pale copies even these.   88

I come across some thing of hers, and pain
stabs me; to flee it feels like fleeing her;
each hour of the day, each place, points her out
to me, and the sorrow or joy each holds: 92
and some there are that picture her in sadness,
others –many more– that show her full of joy.
And there's remorse for the wrongs I did her:
if I could but redress them with my blood!   96

By its effects love makes its presence felt;
quantitatively, it can't be measured;
a lover's worth depends on whom he loves,
the strength of love depends on where it enters.   100
Quality in love depends on likeness,
for love is wont to hanker for the same:
flesh wants flesh, and the soul its equal seeks;
they spawn a bastard child that hates them both.   104

Qui ama carn, perduda carn, no ama,
mas, en membrant lo delit, dol li resta.
En tot amor cau amat e amable;
108 doncs, mort lo cos, aquell qui ell amava
no pot amar, no trobant res que ame;
amor no viu, desig mort i esperança,
i en lo no-res no pot haver espera:
112 quant és del cos la mort a no-res torna.

Si la que am és fora d'aquest segle,
la major part d'aquella és en ésser.
E quan al món en carn ella vivia,
116 son esperit jo volguí amar simple;
e doncs, quant més que en present res no·m torba:
ella vivint, la carn m'era rebel·le.
Los grans contrasts de nostres parts discordes
120 canten forçats acord, e de grat contra.

De mon voler jutge cascú la causa,
e farà poc, veent en mi les obres:
la mia amor per la mort no és morta,
124 ne sent dolor, veent-me lo món perdre.
Jo am e tem ab honesta vergonya
l'esperit sol de la qui Déus perdone,
e res de mi ne del món no cobege,
128 sinó que Déu en lo cel la col·loque.

Tornada

Mare de Déu, si és en purgatori
son esperit, per no purgats delictes,
sí ton fill prec no guard los precs d'on vénen
132 mas lla on van: mos pecats no li noguen!

The love of carnal lovers dies with flesh,
but grief descends with thoughts of pleasure lost.
Lover and beloved make up every love;
so when the body's dead, love has nowhere   108
on which to fix, and the lover cannot love;
lost hope and desire love cannot outlast,
where there is nothingness it cannot reign;
death returns to nothing all that is flesh.   112

Though she has left this world, the finest part
of the woman I love remains here still.
While yet she lived in body on this earth,
her soul unfleshed I sought alone to love;   116
it's easier now the flesh does not obstruct:
while she was here, alive, my flesh rebelled.
Man's discordant parts will sing in chorus
when forced, but then screech gladly out of key.   120

Let each man judge what kind of love is mine:
an easy task, with my actions before him.
Death has been unable to kill my love,
and painlessly I can renounce the flesh.   124
Humbly and purely I love and revere
her spirit (may God have mercy) for itself.
I want nothing for myself or of this world,
only that God will place her in Heaven.   128

Envoi

Mother of God, if purgatory's where
her spirit dwells, atoning for her sins,
ask your Son, to hear, not for me, this prayer,
but for her sake. For my sins don't make her pay!   132

XCV

¿Què val delit, puis no és conegut
ans és fastig quan és molt costumat?
Ço per què mort vós haureu atraçat
4   dins molt breu temps volreu haver perdut;
e ço de què no imaginarem
que·l perdre·ns fos una poca dolor,
si·l cas hi ve, sentim tal amargor
8   que de bon grat vida abandonarem.

En aquest punt me trop jo tan extrem:
ço que volguí ab molt extrema ardor
tornà en mi una llenta calor,
12   e puis, perdut, mortal dolor me prem.
Tal mudament en si hom no veurà
com en mi veig per nostre partiment;
la mort ho fa, qui·m tol mon bé present;
16   del venidor sap Déu lo que serà.

Molts han perdut tot lo que ve e va
—fills, e muller, e part de llur argent—
e resta'ls cor ab null esperdiment,
20   e mai virtut en llur cor habità;
e jo tinc clos e segellat procés
que per null temps delit jo sentiré;
ne planc lo dan per on ma dolor ve,
24   mas l'aspra mort d'on son mal vengut és.

Un poc delit en ma dolor és pres:
ja sent plaer com mon cor mal sosté
pensant per qui ne d'on ma dolor ve;
28   a mi no plau de dolor ser defés.
Oh tu, qui est fora del present món,
e veus a mi per ta mort mal passar,
acapta ab Déu que·m pusques avisar
32   quins esperits a tu de prop te són!

XCV

Set no store by pleasure: taken for granted
when it's ours, too much and soon it irks us,
wishing we were rid of that very thing
for which we'd once have given up our lives;   4
and yet what we assume would cause us not
the slightest pain if we should ever lose it,
fills us with grief so bitter, when it's lost,
that death we'd gladly welcome, if we could.   8

Such is the extreme I must inhabit;
what once I had desired with fiercest ardour
had turned in me to but the gentlest heat;
it's gone, and now I'm gripped by mortal pain.   12
No man could ever be more changed than I
by this parting that wrenched us two apart.
With you Death from my life took all that's good;
God knows alone if future good awaits.   16

What comes and what goes many men have lost
–children, or wives, or some of their fortune–
and such men as these feel no loss at all,
for virtue never dwelt within their hearts;   20
but I hold a covenant, signed and sealed,
that never again will I know delight;
it's not my suffering that I bewail;
rather, the bitter death that is its cause.   24

In all this pain, one pleasure's to be found
that comes each time my heart begins to ache
with thoughts of who and what create the hurt;
let me not be shielded from such pain.   28
Oh you who left this world, and now see me
suffering bitterest grief for your death,
ask God's consent that you may let me know
which kinds of spirits you now dwell amongst!   32

La mort, qui tol lo agradable don
que vida i sort als hòmens volen dar,
quant és de mi m'ha tolt sens mi matar.
36   De mos tres temps me resta lo que fon;
d'aquest present a tothom do ma part,
car no hi ha res que·m vinga en plaer;
del venidor no vull haver esper,
40   puis la tristor és a mi dolç esguard.

No·m dolré tant que en dolor sia fart,
ans ma dolor jo prenc per mon mester;
mon cor de carn és pus fort que l'acer,
44   puis ell és viu i entre nós és depart.
Quan l'esperit del cos li viu partir,
e li doní lo darrer besar fred,
conec de mi que amor no·m té son dret,
48   que ab cor sencer ho posquí sostenir.

En molt breu temps l'hom no·s pot dolorir
tant com depuis: ab l'entendre és costret,
car per gran torb tots comptes no ha fet.
52   Dolor vol temps si l'hom tot l'ha sentir,
e majorment com raó hi apareix,
car, si no ho fa, tost s'hi mescla conhort.
Massa és foll lo qui·s fa tan gran tort
56   si cascun jorn son dol foll no pereix.

No·m jutge algú si primer no coneix
si tinc raó per dolre'm d'esta mort:
en ella fon complit lo meu deport;
60   ella finint, lo món per mi feneix.
¿Qui és tan cruel que no·s dolga de si
e de aquell qui en part més que si vol?
Doncs, si algú pusque fer honest dol,
64   llicenciat no·l fon més que a mi.

Oh mort, qui fas l'hom venturós mesquí,
i el ple de goig, tu mitjançant, se dol!
De tu ha por tot quant és jus lo sol;
68   dolor, sens tu, no hauria camí.

Death, which takes from man that pleasurable gift
that life and fortune have bestowed on him,
has taken everything except my breath.
Of time's three tenses, I've only what is past;   36
as for my present, all are welcome to it,
since I take joy in nothing it contains;
for the future I would sooner hold no hope;
the sweetest prospect sadness seems to me.   40

Pain in this grieving shall never have its fill;
as much I'll suffer as my need dictates;
this heart of flesh must be stronger than steel,
since, even though we're parted, it beats on.   44
When I saw the spirit had abandoned
her body, and I gave her the last, cold kiss,
I knew that love in me held no dominion,
since I could bear all this, my heart intact.   48

At once man cannot grieve as he later must;
his own understanding will constrain him,
and his perplexity amidst events.
Grief's full effect will only come with time,   52
especially when reason intervenes,
or else consolation would soon set in.
Grief will shrink in men with each passing day,
save when it has tipped them into madness.   56

Let no one judge me before he's pondered
the reasons why over this death I grieve:
in her there was contained my every joy;
now that she's dead, this world holds nothing more.   60
Most cruel he'd be who didn't grieve the loss
of one he loved more almost than himself.
So, if it's virtuous justly to grieve,
no man had ever greater right than I.   64

Oh death, who wretched makes the fortunate man,
and fills with woe whoever lives in joy!
You are feared by all that lives beneath the sun;
pain, without you, could find no path to man.   68

Tu est d'amor son enemic mortal,
faent partir los coratges units.
Ab ton colp cert has morts los meus delits;
72   gustar no·s pot bé ton amargós mal.

Tornada

Tu, esperit, si mon ben fet te val,
la sang daré per tos goigs infinits.
Vine a mi de dia o de nits;
76   fes-me saber si pregar per tu cal.

You are the mortal enemy of love,
two hearts dividing that had long been one.
With one sure blow you've killed in me all joy;
none can lightly bear the bitter ill you wreak.   72

Envoi

Spirit, if it only could suffice, my blood
shall be the price of your eternal bliss.
Come to me, either by night or by day,
and tell me that you're not beyond all prayers.   76

XCVI

LA GRAN DOLOR que llengua no pot dir
del qui·s veu mort e no sap on irà
(no sap son Déu si per a si·l volrà
4   o si en l'infern lo volrà sebollir):
semblant dolor lo meu esperit sent,
no sabent què de vós Déus ha ordenat,
car vostre bé o mal a mi és dat;
8   del que haureu jo·n seré sofirent.

Tu, esperit, qui has fet partiment
ab aquell cos qual he jo tant amat,
veges a mi qui so passionat.
12   Dubtant estic fer-te raonament:
lo lloc on est me farà canviar
d'enteniment de ço que·t volré dir.
Goig o tristor per tu he jo complir;
16   en tu està quant Déu me volrà dar.

Pregant a Déu, les mans no·m cal plegar,
car fet és tot quant li pot avenir:
si és e·l cel, no·s pot lo bé espremir;
20   si en infern, en foll és mon pregar.
Si és així, anul·la'm l'esperit;
sia tornat mon ésser en no-res,
e majorment si en lloc tal per mi és;
24   no sia jo de tant adolorit.

No sé què dir que·m fartàs d'haver dit;
si crit o call, no trop qui·m satisfés;
si vac o pens, he temps en va despés:
28   de tot quant faç, ans de fer me penit.
No planc lo dan de mon delit perdut,
tanta és la por que·m ve de son gran mal:
tot mal és poc si no és perpetual,
32   e tem aquest no l'haja merescut.

XCVI

THE FEARFUL anguish that no tongue can tell
when, after death, a man must learn his fate
(will God now unto his bosom take him,
or else decide to bury him in Hell?),   4
now torment such as this afflicts my soul,
dreading the end that God for you ordained:
your fate, will also, good or ill, be mine;
whichever it is, I shall suffer it too.   8

You, spirit, who now have taken your leave
of the body that I have loved so much,
can you see me here and the pain I bear?
With you I would speak, though I dread your words,   12
for everything I have to say depends
on what place it is your soul inhabits.
Sadness or joy I will attain through you;
to you is tied all God intends for me.   16

In vain I clench my hands in prayer: all that
could happen has already come to pass.
If in Heaven, joy ineffable is hers;
if she's in Hell, then foolish are my prayers.   20
If that's the case, annihilate my soul,
and turn my being back to nothingness,
especially if because of me she's damned;
with suffering so cruel do not afflict me.   24

There are no words that, spoken, do not fail;
my silence and my cries are both in vain;
I clear my mind, or let it fill with thoughts:
no use –regret attends my every act;   28
so great are my fears that she's in torment,
I scarcely grieve for pleasure I have lost:
suffering eternal trivial makes our pain–
and such is the punishment I fear she earned.   32

Lo dan mortal és molt més que temut,
e tol-ne part ésser a tots egual.
Oh tu, dolor, sies-me cominal:
36   en contra oblit vulles-me ser escut.
Fir-me lo cor e tots los senys me pren,
farta't en mi, car no·m defens de tu;
dóna'm tant mal que me'n planga cascú;
40   tant com tu pots, lo teu poder m'estén.

Tornada

Tu, esperit, si res no te'n defén,
romp lo costum que dels morts és comú:
torna en lo món, e mostra què és de tu.
44   Lo teu esguard no·m donarà espavén.

No greater fear has man than the havoc
death wreaks, impartial with us all, but no less
dreadful. Oh pain, if you'd but treat me fairly:
become my shield to guard against forgetting,   36
pierce my heart, seize hold of all my senses;
spend all your rage, I'll offer no defence.
Give me such pain that everyone will grieve,
and let your strength work all it can in me.   40

Envoi

You, spirit, if there's nothing to prevent you,
break just this once the customs of the dead:
come back to the world, and tell me of your fate;
I'll feel no terror at the sight of you.   44

XCVII

Si per null temps creguí ser amador,
en mi conec d'amor poc sentiment.
Si mi compar al comú de la gent,
és veritat que en mi trop gran amor,
però si guard algú del temps passat,
i el que amor pot fer en lloc dispost,
nom d'amador solament no m'acost,
car tant com dec no só passionat.

Morta és ja la que tant he amat,
mas jo son viu, veent ella morir;
ab gran amor no·s pot bé soferir
que d'ella mort me pusca haver llunyat.
Lla dec anar on és lo seu camí;
no sé què·m té que en açò no m'acord:
sembla que ho vull, mas no és ver, puis mort
res no la tol al qui la vol per si.

¿En què restà que vida no finí
com prop la mort jo la viu acostar,
dient, plorant, «No vullau mi lleixar,
hajau dolor de la dolor de mi»?
Oh cor malvat d'aquell qui·s veu tal cas
com pecejat o sens sang no roman!
Molt poca amor e pietat molt gran
degra bastar que senyal gran mostràs.

¿Qui serà aquell que en dolre abastàs,
lo piadós mal de la mort vengut?
Oh cruel mal, qui tols la joventut,
e fas podrir les carns dins en lo vas!
L'esperit, ple de paor, volant va
a l'incert lloc, tement l'eternal dan;
tot lo delit present deçà roman.
¿Qui és lo sant qui de mort no dubtà?

XCVII

I THOUGHT I knew, before, what true love was,
but now it's clear I didn't have a clue.
When I consider how most people are,
it's true that love in me is very strong,   4
but if I think of those from long ago,
of all that love can in true lovers work,
then such I have no right to call myself:
far short of the mark my suffering falls.   8

The woman I so greatly loved is dead,
but even though I watched her die, I live;
so great's my love, it hardly can be borne
that we two should be wrenched apart by death.   12
Now should I follow too that selfsame road;
I do not know what weakens my resolve;
I think I want this, yet it can't be true:
nothing can prevent a death that is desired.   16

How can it be my own life did not end
when I watched her drawing close to death,
and in tears begged her: 'Do not leave me here,
only take pity on my piteous grief'?   20
Oh wretched the man whose heart does not break
at such an hour, or is drained of all its blood;
true sorrow, even where there's little love,
should always leave great marks of bitter grief.   24

Yet who could ever grieve as he would wish
when the pitiful pain of death's upon him?
Oh cruellest ill, which snatches youth away
and leaves the flesh to rot within the grave!   28
The spirit, filled with terror, flies away
it knows not where, but dreads damnation;
the world's delights it now must leave behind.
What saint has never lived in fear of death?   32

¿Qui serà aquell qui la mort planyerà,
d'altre o de si, tant com és lo gran mal?
Sentir no·s pot lo damnatge mortal;
36   molt menys lo sap qui mort jamés temptà.
Oh cruel mal, donant departiment
per tots los temps als coratges units!
Mos sentiments me trop esbalaïts;
40   mon esperit no té son sentiment.

Tots mos amics hagen complanyiment
de mi, segons veuran ma passió;
haja delit lo meu fals companyó
44   e l'envejós qui de mal delit sent.
Car, tant com puc, jo·m dolc e dolre'm vull
e com no·m dolc, assats pas desplaer,
car jo desig que perdés tot plaer
48   e que jamés cessàs plorar mon ull.

Tan poc no am que ma cara no mull
d'aigua de plor, sa vida e mort pensant:
en tristor visc, de la vida membrant,
52   e de sa mort aitant com puc me dull.
No bast en més, en mi no pusc fer pus
sinó obeir lo que ma dolor vol;
ans perdre vull la raó si la'm tol.
56   Mas, pus no muir, de poca amor m'acús.

Tornada

Tot amador d'amar poc no s'excús
que sia viu, e mort lo seu amat,
o que del món almenys visca apartat,
60   que solament haja nom de resclús.

Can we lament a death as it deserves,
whether another's or that which waits for us?
Our senses cannot grasp its calamity;
if it never touched us, even less we know.   36
Oh cruel death, for all eternity
two hearts parting that had always been one!
Stupefied all my senses seem to be;
my spirit's drained of everything it felt.   40

When they see what great suffering is mine,
all who love me will be moved to pity,
while false friends will rejoice, the envious too,
who always in another's pain delight.   44
I grieve, and still shall grieve as deeply
as I can, wretched when I do not grieve;
every pleasure I would gladly discard,
and have tears flow incessant from my eyes.   48

I can't help drenching my face with tears, to think
how she lived and died: my love extends so far.
I live in sadness, remembering her life,
and over her death all I can I grieve.   52
I am incapable of more than this;
I can do only what suffering dictates;
sooner I'd go mad than renounce my pain.
Yet I still live; of that my love's accused.   56

Envoi

Love insufficient is the charge whenever
lovers, even though their loved one's dead, live on;
the least they can do is give up the world,
and in reclusion then live out their lives.   60

A POEM ON GOD AND PREDESTINATION

CV

Puis que sens tu, algú a tu no basta,
dóna'm la mà o pels cabells me lleva;
si no estenc la mia envers la tua,
quasi forçat a tu mateix me tira.
Jo vull anar envers tu a l'encontre;
no sé per què no faç lo que volria,
puis jo son cert haver voluntat franca,
e no sé què aquest voler m'empatxa.

Llevar mi vull, e prou no m'hi esforce;
ço fa lo pes de mes terribles colpes.
Ans que la mort lo procés a mi cloga,
plàcia't, Déu, puis teu vull ser, que ho vulles;
fes que ta sang mon cor dur amollesca:
de semblant mal guarí ella a molts altres.
Ja lo tardar ta ira·m denuncia:
ta pietat no troba en mi què obre.

Tan clarament en l'entendre no peque
com lo voler he carregat de colpa.
Ajuda'm, Déu! Mas, follament te pregue,
car tu no vals sinó al qui s'ajuda,
e tots aquells qui a tu se apleguen
no·ls pots fallir, e mostren-ho tos braces.
¿Què faré jo, que no meresc m'ajudes,
car tant com puc conec que no m'esforce?

Perdona mi si follament te parle:
de passió parteixen mes paraules.
Jo sent paor d'infern, al qual faç via;
girar-la vull, e no hi disponc mos passos.
Mas jo·m record que meritist lo lladre;
tant quant hom veu no hi bastaven ses obres:
ton esperit lla on li plau espira;
com ne per què, no sap qui en carn visca.

CV

SINCE WE MAY reach you only by your will,
give me your hand, else wrench me by the hair;
if up to yours I fail to stretch my hand,
drag me to you; take, if I resist, no heed.   4
There I want to go where you await me;
I don't know why I can't do what I wish:
that I possess free will I do not doubt;
something obstructs it; what, I do not know.   8

I pull myself up, but every time sink down
under the weight of my terrible sins.
Lord, before my case by death's forever closed,
accept me as your own, who long for you;   12
send your blood to melt my hardened heart:
many it has cured of the same disease.
But your delay alone proclaims your ire;
in me your mercy falls on stony ground.   16

Less I have sinned with my understanding
than with my will, which I've weighed down with guilt.
Help me, my God! But foolish is my plea,
for you help only those who help themselves;   20
yet, who come unto you, they shall not want,
and your arms are ever offered to us.
But what of me, who drag my feet, and know
I've nothing done that could deserve your help?   24

Forgive me if folly is all I say;
the passions force out every word I speak:
I live in fear of Hell, but there direct
my steps; I would turn back, and yet can not.   28
But that you saved the thief I don't forget:
to our eyes, more than his works deserved.
Wheresoever it wills your spirit breathes;
when it breathes, or why, none of us can tell.   32

Ab tot que só mal crestià per obra,
ira no·t tinc, ne de res no t'encolpe.
Jo són tot cert que per tostemps bé obres
36   e fas tant bé donant mort com la vida:
tot és egual quant surt de ta potença.
D'on tinc per foll qui vers tu·s vol iréixer;
amor de mal, e de bé ignorança
40   és la raó que·ls hòmens no·t coneixen.

A tu deman que lo cor m'enfortesques,
sí que·l voler ab ta voluntat lligue,
e puis que sé que lo món no·m profita,
44   dóna'm esforç que del tot l'abandone;
e lo delit que·l bon hom de tu gusta
fes-me'n sentir una poca centilla,
perquè ma carn, qui m'està molt rebel·le,
48   haja afalac, que del tot no·m contraste.

Ajuda'm, Déu!, que sens tu no·m puc moure,
per què·l meu cos és més que paralític.
Tant són en mi envellits los mals hàbits,
52   que la virtut al gustar m'és amarga.
Oh Déu, mercé! Revolta'm ma natura
que mala és per la mia gran colpa.
E si per mort jo puc rembre ma falta,
56   esta serà ma dolça penitença.

Jo tem a tu més que no·t só amable,
e davant tu confés la colpa aquesta.
Torbada és la mia esperança,
60   e dintre mi sent terrible baralla:
jo veig a tu just e misericorde,
veig ton voler qui sens mèrits gracia;
dónes e tols de grat lo do, sens mèrits.
64   ¿Qual és tan just, quant més jo, que no tema?

Si Job lo just por de Déu l'opremia,
¿què faré jo que dins les colpes nade?
Com pens d'infern, que temps no s'hi esmenta,
68   lla és mostrat tot quant sentiments temen.

Though a bad Christian, as my works proclaim,
anger or resentment I bear you none.
I have firm faith that all you do is good,
and that you do good both when you give life   36
or death; all is one that comes from your might.
Only a fool would be angry with you;
love of evil and ignorance of good
–if men don't know you, there's the reason why.   40

All I ask is that you strengthen my heart,
so my desires with your will become fused;
the world, I know, cannot profit me at all:
give me strength to reject it utterly;   44
fire me with some small spark of that delight
a good man feels when he thinks of you,
and then my greatly rebellious flesh
will be appeased, and give me some respite.   48

Help me, Lord, for I cannot take a step
without you, paralysed my limbs, or worse.
Old habits are so deep ingrained in me
that virtue's taken on a bitter taste.   52
Lord, have mercy, and reverse my nature,
made evil with the heavy weight of sin.
And if my sins can be redeemed by death,
then that sweet penitence I'll gladly make.   56

My fear of you is greater than my love;
this heavy sin before you I confess.
My hope is all confounded; within me
I feel a dreadful battle raging on: 60
I see that you are merciful and just,
that, heedless of merits, your will grants grace;
as you may choose, the gift is granted or denied.
Shall I not tremble, when even good men fear?   64

If fear of God weighed upon righteous Job,
what then of me, floundering in my sins?
I think of Hell, where time has no meaning,
and feel as much terror as man can know.   68

L'arma, qui és contemplar Déu eleta,
en contra aquell, blasfemant, se rebel·la:
no és en hom de tan gran mal estima.
72   Doncs, ¿com està qui vers tal part camina?

Prec-te, Senyor, que la vida m'abreuges,
ans que pejors casos a mi enseguesquen.
En dolor visc, faent vida perversa,
76   e tem dellà la mort per tostemps llonga.
Doncs, mal deçà, e dellà mal sens terme.
Pren-me al punt que millor en mi trobes;
lo detardar no sé a què·m servesca.
80   No té repòs lo qui té fer viatge.

Jo·m dolc perquè tant com vull no·m puc dolre
de l'infinit damnatge, lo qual dubte,
e tal dolor no la recull natura
84   ne·s pot asmar e menys sentir pot l'home.
E doncs, açò sembla a mi flaca excusa
com de mon dan tant com és no m'espante;
si·l cel deman no li do basta estima;
88   fretura pas de por e d'esperança.

Per bé que tu irascible te mostres,
ço és defalt de nostra ignorança:
lo teu voler tostemps guarda clemença,
92   ton semblant mal és bé inestimable.
Perdona'm, Déu, si t'he donada colpa,
car jo confés ésser aquell colpable;
ab ull de carn he fets los teus judicis.
96   Vulles dar llum a la vista de l'arma!

Lo meu voler al teu és molt contrari,
e·m só enemic, pensant-me amic ésser.
Ajuda'm, Déu, puis me veus en tal pressa!
100   Jo·m desesper si los mèrits meus guardes;
jo m'enuig molt la vida com allongue
e dubte molt que aquella fenesca.
En dolor visc, car mon desig no·s ferma,
104   e ja en mi alterat és l'arbitre.

The soul, to contemplate our God predestined,
rebels against him with blasphemous thoughts;
none can imagine the torments of Hell.
How should he feel who walks along that road?   72

Put an end, Lord, I beg you, to my life,
before I have time to do even worse.
I groan in pain at my perversity,
and fear eternal death beyond this life.   76
Here only pain, and there pain without end
awaits me. Take me when I'm at my best;
it avails me not to put that moment off.
The journey awaits; there is no time to rest.   80

I grieve that as I should I do not grieve,
knowing eternally I may be damned;
the pain I fear is not in nature found;
man cannot guess at it, nor much less feel.   84
This is some excuse, but, I think, a weak one,
if my fear far short of my peril falls;
I ask for Heaven, yet little prize it;
fear it is that fails me, no less than hope.   88

Whenever you seem to us to be angry,
this only is our ignorance at fault;
your will shows clemency in all it does;
what we think bad is ineffable good.   92
Forgive me, Lord, if ever I accused you,
for I confess myself the guilty one;
I have judged all you do with eyes of flesh.
Only give light to the eyes of my soul!   96

All I do is contrary to your will,
my own false friend, enemy to myself.
Help me, Lord, since you see me in these straits!
That you'll judge my merits brings me to despair;   100
I loathe each passing day my life goes on,
and yet I dread its coming to an end.
I live in anguish, with no firm intent:
even now in me I sense a change of will.   104

Tu est la fi on totes fins termenen,
e no és fi si en tu no termena.
Tu est lo bé on tot altre·s mesura,
108		e no és bo qui a tu, Déu, no sembla.
Al qui·t complau tu aquell déu nomenes;
per tu semblar, major grau d'home·l muntes;
d'on és gran dret del qui plau al diable
112		prenga lo nom d'aquell ab qui·s conforma.

Alguna fi en aquest món se troba;
ne és vera fi, puis que no fa l'hom fèlix:
és lo començ per on l'altra s'acaba,
116		segons lo córs que entendre pot un home.
Los filosofs qui aquella posaren
en si mateixs són ésser vists discordes:
senyal és cert que en veritat no·s funda;
120		per consegüent a l'home no contenta.

Bona per si no fon la llei judaica
(en paradís per ella no s'entrava),
mas tant com fon començ d'aquesta nostra,
124		de què·s pot dir d'aquestes dues una.
Així la fi de tot en tot humana
no da repòs a l'apetit, o terme;
mas tampoc l'hom sens ella no ha l'altra:
128		Sant Joan fon senyalant lo Messies.

No té repòs qui nulla altra fi guarda,
car en res àls lo voler no reposa:
ço sent cascú, e no hi cal subtilesa,
132		que, fora tu, lo voler no s'atura.
Sí com los rius a la mar tots acorren,
així les fins totes en tu se n'entren.
Puis te conec, esfortça'm que jo t'ame:
136		vença l'amor a la por que jo·t porte.

E si amor tanta com vull no m'entra,
creix-me la por, sí que, tement, no peque,
car, no pecant, jo perdré aquells hàbits
140		que són estats per què no t'am la causa.

You are the end in which all ends must meet,
there is no end that does not lead to you.
You are the good by which all good is gauged,
and none is good unless he is like you.   108
Whomever you please you turn into a god,
in your likeness raised to man's highest rung;
it follows, then: who keeps the Devil pleased
will take the name of he whose ways he chose.   112

This life has its worldly ends to offer,
and none of them true, that lead man to bliss;
where the world's good ends, there true good begins,
as far as men can understand such things.   116
Some philosophers claim this world contains
true good, but each the other contradicts
–an infallible sign it holds no truth;
that's why such good cannot make man content.   120

In itself the Law of Moses held no good
(Paradise could not be entered by that route),
but it was the beginning of our own,
so one might say that these two form one Law.   124
Just so, that end which human will desires
leaves restless appetite to go unchecked,
yet none without it reach that other end:
Saint John was sent to prophesize our Lord.   128

Whoever other than the true end seeks
can never have respite: elsewhere our will
cannot rest –this each simple fool will know–
but man's desires in you can find an end.   132
Just as all rivers rush down to the sea,
so every end must finally meet in you.
Since I know what you are, to love of you
compel me; make love vanquish all my fear.   136

But if I fail to love as I would wish,
heap up my fear, and so let dread hold sin
at bay; then, free of sin, shall I shrug off
those habits that have barred the way to love.   140

Muiren aquells qui de tu m'apartaren,
puis m'han mig mort e·m tolen que no visca.
Oh Senyor Déu!, fes que la vida allargue,
144   puis me apar que envers tu jo m'acoste.

¿Qui·m mostrarà davant tu fer excusa
quan hauré dar mon mal ordenat compte?
Tu m'has donat disposició recta,
148   e jo he fet del regle falç molt corba;
dreçar-la vull, mas he mester ta ajuda.
Ajuda'm, Déu!, car ma força és flaca.
Desig saber què de mi predestines.
152   A tu és present, i a mi causa venible.

No·t prec que·m dons sanitat de persona,
ne béns alguns de natura i fortuna,
mas solament que a tu, Déu, sols ame,
156   car jo só cert que·l major bé s'hi causa.
Per consegüent, delectació alta
jo no la sent, per no dispost sentir-la;
mas, per saber, un home grosser jutja
160   que·l major bé sus tots és delitable.

¿Qual serà·l jorn que la mort jo no tema?
E serà quan de ta amor jo m'inflame;
e no·s pot fer sens menyspreu de la vida
164   e que per tu aquella jo menyspree.
Lladoncs seran jus mi totes les coses
que de present me veig sobre los muscles;
lo qui no tem del fort lleó les ungles
168   molt menys tembrà lo fibló de la vespa.

Prec-te, Senyor, que·m fasses insensible
e que en null temps alguns delits jo senta,
no solament los lleigs qui·t vénen contra,
172   mas tots aquells que indiferents se troben.
Açò desig perquè sol en tu pense
e pusca haver la via que en tu·s dreça.
Fes-ho, Senyor, e si per temps me'n torne,
176   haja per cert trobar ta aurella sorda.

May Death strike those who from you estranged me,
stifled all life, and left me almost dead!
Lord God, oh yet a while please let me live:
Even now I feel I'm drawing near you.   144

How will I excuse myself before you
when my disordered reckoning I make?
From birth you disposed me to be upright,
but the straight rule I've bent into a scythe;   148
I would set it true again, but your aid
I need. Oh, help me, Lord, for I languish.
Let me learn in what way I'm predestined,
your divine present, but my future fate.   152

Lord, I do not ask for bodily health,
nor of nature or of fortune some good,
but only that I may love you alone;
from such love derives the highest good.   156
And so must it be that heavenly joy
I cannot feel since such I was created;
yet with understanding a fool will see
the highest good brings joy above all else.   160

When will be the day I'll lose my fear of death?
It will be when with love of you I burn;
but in contempt I must first hold my life
and must for your sake only feel such scorn.   164
Then shall I crush beneath my feet those things
that weigh –this heavy burden– on my back;
he who has no dread of the lion's fierce claws
will laugh off the sting of the tiny wasp.   168

Lord, I beg that you deaden my senses
and from certain pleasures turn me for good,
not just foul delights that most offend you
but also those which lead to venial sins.   172
Thus will all my thoughts be only of you,
and I'll take that road leading where you are.
Only do this, Lord, and if I turn back,
may your ears to me stay deaf for ever.   176

Tol-me dolor com me veig perdre·l segle
car mentre·m dolc tant com vull jo no t'ame,
e vull-ho fer, mas l'hàbit me contrasta:
180　　en temps passat me carreguí la colpa.
Tant te cost jo com molts qui no·t serviren,
e tu·ls has fet no menys que jo·t demane,
per què·t suplic que dins lo cor tu m'entres,
184　　puix est entrat en pus abominable.

Catòlic só, mas la fe no m'escalfa
que la fredor lenta dels senys apague,
car jo eleix ço que mos sentiments senten,
188　　e paradís crec per fe i raó jutge.
Aquella part de l'esperit és prompta,
mas la dels senys rossegant la m'acoste.
Doncs tu, Senyor, ab foc de fe m'acorre
192　　tant que la part que·m porta fred abrase.

Tu creïst mi perquè l'ànima salve,
e pot-se fer de mi saps lo contrari.
Si és així, ¿per què, doncs, me creaves,
196　　puix fon en tu lo saber infal·lible?
Torna a no-res, jo·t suplic, lo meu ésser,
car més me val que tostemps l'escur càrcer.
Jo crec a tu com volguist dir de Judes
200　　que·l fóra bo no fos nat al món home.

Per mi segur, havent rebut baptisme,
no fos tornat als braços de la vida,
mas a la mort hagués retut lo deute,
204　　e de present jo no viuria en dubte.
Major dolor d'infern los hòmens senten
que los delits de paraís no jutgen;
lo mal sentit és d'aquell altre exemple,
208　　e paradís sens lo sentir se jutja.

Dóna'm esforç que prenga de mi venge:
jo·m trop ofés contra tu ab gran colpa.
E si no hi bast, tu de ma carn te farta,
212　　ab que no·m tocs l'esperit, que a tu sembla.

I grieve to see my life draw near its end;
yet, for all my grief, I cannot love you
–not as I would: habit is against me,
and I am burdened with such weight of guilt.   180
Many did not serve you, yet you have done
for them no less than what I ask for me;
I beg you, Lord, to come into my heart,
since some you entered more vile still than mine.   184

Christian I am, and yet the warmth of faith
can never melt my senses' lingering chill,
and these I follow in everything I do;
my faith's in Heaven, which reason confirms.   188
My spirit's in readiness; but I must drag
the body where my other part awaits.
Send, Lord, the fire of faith to succour me,
and let it scorch the part that's set in ice.   192

You created me that I might save my soul,
yet you may know a contrary fate is mine.
If this is so, then why was I created,
since your omniscience embraces all?   196
Return, I beg, to nothingness my being:
sooner this than that dark, eternal cell.
I believe in you who of Judas said
better had it been that man had not been born.   200

If only, baptised into salvation,
to the arms of life I hadn't been returned,
but there and then I'd paid my due to death,
I wouldn't know this present life of fear.   204
Men more quickly grasp the torments of Hell,
than ever can imagine Heaven's bliss;
the pain we feel's a copy of that other,
but we must guess at Paradise, unfelt.   208

Give me strength to take revenge upon myself;
your will I've offended with my great sins.
But if I fail, wreak vengeance on my flesh,
my soul unharmed, that's in your likeness made.   212

E sobretot ma fe que no vacil·le,
e no tremol la mia esperança;
no·m fallirà caritat, elles fermes.
216   E de la carn, si·t suplic, no me n'oges.

¿Oh quan serà que regaré les galtes
d'aigua de plor ab les llàgremes dolces?
Contrició és la font d'on emanen;
220   aquesta és clau que·l cel tancat nos obre;
d'atrició parteixen les amargues
perquè en temor més que en amor se funden.
Mas, tals quals són, d'aquestes me abunda,
224   puix són camí e via per les altres.

Faith, above all, unwavering must be,
and hope must never tremble; charity
then will not fail me, if these two are firm.
Turn a deaf ear to my pleas for the flesh.   216

Oh when shall I be able to feel sweet
tears of repentance coursing down my cheeks?
Contrition is the fount from which these flow,
the key that opens Heaven's bolted door.   220
I weep from attrition these bitter tears
since they spring more from fear of you than love;
yet even these in abundance send me,
to those other tears the path and sure road.   224

NOTES

LOVE POEMS

I

This poem develops through a series of similes a theme found commonly in medieval literature: the pain of remembering past happiness from the perspective of a wretched present. The topic has its roots in Boethius (*De Consolatione Philosophiae*, II, 4) and has its most famous expression in Dante (*Inferno*, V, 121-123), a poet whose work March certainly knew.

43 *starve*. I have introduced a metaphor not in March's text; yet 'contrasta' (a rhyme word) clearly refers to constancy's opposition to the worm, so that 'starve' is not outside the connotative range of March's verb.

44 'these envious tongues' refers to the troudadouresque concept of the *lauzengiers* who seek to uncover and expose the illicit courtly liaison.

IV

7 Here the 'two women' loved by the poet represent woman as the object of physical desire, and woman as the object of a form of love in which the spirit has a major role. This meaning of the phrase is clear from the following stanzas.

V

9-16 The idea that part of Christ's reasons for coming into the world as man was to deceive the Devil appears in the Apocrypha.

VII

67-68 March cites a specific river, the Segre, in a rhyme position; it is unlikely that any special meaning is meant to attach to this particular river, and I have not felt obliged to import it as an exoticism into the translation, chosing instead to de-particularize.

XI

16 March's *rigor*, a rhyme word, is translated as 'touch' (the touch of death); the exact meaning is 'cruelty', 'harshness'.

XIII

4 The 'great tales' to which March refers are probably jongleuresque recitals of versions of the great medieval romances.

13-14 These lines refer to Janus of Lusignan, the Christian king of Cyprus who was taken captive by the sultan Barsbey on 5 July 1426. He was subjected to great humiliation and held prisoner for eight months until a huge ransom was paid, partly by the Vatican with money from Spain. Janus's defeat had a demoralizing effect on the Mediterranean Christian countries for some time afterwards.

17-20 The giant Tityos was sent to Hades after trying to rape Diana where, according to Virgil, a vulture fed eternally on his liver.

XVIII

17 I have extended the metaphor of line 18; *substance*: there is an implicit contrast with 'accident'; both these Scholastic terms also appear in XCII, 191-192.

33-34 Numerous accounts of the miracles of St Paul circulated in the Middle Ages, and some of them appear in the Apocrypha.

41 The 'philosopher' who throws all his possessions into the sea is variously identified in a number of accounts as Diogenes, Socrates or Crates the Cynic.

49 Natural or physical philosophy was the object of criticism by Christian authors from Augustine onwards (*City of God*, VIII, 1-8), although there were forms of it in the Middle Ages, as well as a Catalan translation of one of the texts, William of Conches's *Dragmaticon*.

XXIX

The image of the simile seems to be taken from Virgil's Georgics, III, 219-236; it also appears in Lucan's *Pharsalia*.

6 *gest*: 'mien' would be a closer but now antiquated rendition; here 'beauty' is used, even though it does not have the connotations of active stance or look that *gest* contains.

XXXIX

This poem, with its refrence to the poet's *oeuvre* in its first line, appeared at the head of some sixteen century manuscripts and editions, and seems to have been taken by the editors of that century to epitomize March's love poetry.

XLVI

There have been several attempts to identify the course of the voyage described by March in the first stanza. If not purely literary in nature, the crossing seems to be East to West across the Mediterranean, suggesting the return from an undocumented visit to the Kingdom of Naples. The voyage takes on Biblical dimensions in the second stanza, in which March describes an apocalyptic scene.

9 The 'pot of stew' (*cassola en forn*) refers to a dish cooking in the baker's oven, which was available to the public for such purposes. There are reminiscences in the same line of Job 41.22 and of Ramon Llull's *Doctrina pueril.*

18 The reference is to votive offerings of wax, such as can still be seen in country churches in Spain and elsewhere.

19-20 It was not uncommon for passengers in peril on the sea to make their confessions to each other if no priest was present.

60 The reference to games of dice probably carries a moral charge, as gambling was decried with great effect by preachers in Valencia in the first half of the fifteenth century, and thousands of games of dice were publicly burned.

LXIV

7-8 The nightingale is a bird emblematic of love in troubadour poetry, often one of the features of the pleasance (*locus amoenus*) in which the poet sings of his love.

25-27 The hunting metaphors stress the poet's declared incompetence in love.

28 The service of the Easter Passion here serves as a metaphor for the poet's own sense of his tragic position.

LXVIII

A further strophe, positioned between the first and second stanzas, appears in an edition of March's work of 1555. There is no definitive evidence that it is by March, but nor can it be discounted entirely as spurious, in spite of the untypical repetitions it contains of phrases from the first stanza.

> ¿Com se farà que visca sens dolor,
> tenint perdut lo bé que posseïa?
> Clar e molt bé ho veu, si no ha follia,
> que mai porà tenir estat millor.
> Doncs, ¿qué farà, puix altre bé no·l resta,
> sinó plorar lo bé del temps perdut?
> Veent molt clar per si ser decebut,
> mai trobarà qui·l faça millor festa.

> *How will he ever live without regret,*
> *now he has lost the good that once was his?*
> *He'd have to be a fool to fail to see*
> *that he will never find a better place.*
> *What, then, is left for him to do but weep*
> *for all the good things he has left behind?*
> *How wrong he was too clearly now he sees:*
> *more pampered than before he'll never be.*

POEMS OF PRAISE AND BLAME

XXIII

1 By 'troubadours' March means 'other poets', since *trobador* was the term used commonly to denote one who wrote verse. Nevertheless, here I have translated the term as 'troubadours' because of its connotative association in English with a particular type of love-poetry–as it happens, precisely the one from which March disassociates himself in this line and in other poems.

12-16 The metaphors are taken from the cloth trade, a very important business in Valencia where there were major importers from Italy, and fortunes were made.

28 *Lady Teresa*: there have been some inconclusive attempts to identify the lady in question. In this poem at least, Lady Teresa seems to be identifiable with 'Lily among thorns', but it is not necessarily the case that all the thirty-

five poems with this pseudonym for the addressed lady can be related to Lady Teresa, whoever she was.

33 The first half of the fifteenth century was a period of great stability for Venice, the 'Serenissima Repubblica', something which the Venetians attributed to the virtues of their Constitution.

XLII

1-8 The turtle-dove is cited in many medieval bestiaries as the natural example of fidelity; see, for instance, T. H. White, *The Book of Beasts* (Gloucester: Sutton, 1984), pp. 145-146. The comparison may possibly carry the implication that *Na Monboí* is a widow (the widow of a member of the knightly class, as line 11 suggests), or simply the former mistress of such a man, perhaps deceased. It is important to bear in mind that, although March implies in line 43 that there had been a personal relationship between him and the woman, the 'noble flesh' mentioned in l. 11 is probably a fellow knight rather than March himself.

12 It has been argued convincingly that there is a pun on the name here (*Jo-a'n* from *Joan*), read in a way that suggests the vulgar ostentation of newly gained wealth (something like 'John's the name, and there's plenty more where that came from'). The name almost certainly is that of a real person, like the name of the woman, *Na Monboí*. If the names did not represent real people, there would not be much point in making this kind of public attack. Lacking an equivalent in English for the Catalan pun, I have chosen instead to use a name for Joan which plays up the accusation against the lady of sexual excess.

18 The implication is that the merchant Joan thinks that, by means of his liaison with *Na Monboí*, he will benefit socially, given her apparent connection. March, from his position in the knightly class, attacks Joan for his social status as a merchant, although, if he was selling the costly Florentine cloth (l. 16), he would have to have been a member of a merchant family of considerable wealth and power (indeed one of the mid-sixteenth century manuscripts gives Joan's surname as 'Junyent', which coincides with that of an enormously influential family of Barcelona cloth merchants, with interests in Valencia).

28 It was a medical belief in March's time that the feminine organism had the capacity to produce poison, especially if the woman engaged in coitus during menstruation (by which the natural poison was purged) or during

lactation; see Danielle Jacquart & Claude Thomasset, *Sexuality and Medicine in the Middle Ages,* trans. Matthew Adamson (Oxford: Polity Press, 1988), Chapter 2. March implies that the woman's lust is such that she engages in sexual activity during the proscribed periods. Her hairiness is a visible sign of her poisoned condition: Na Monboí suffers from an excess of unpurged bodily superfluities which, as in animals, manifest themselves partly in the form of hairs.

33 Here March projects further into *Na Monboí's* future, foreseeing a later stage in which she will make a living as a professional procuress.

PHILOSOPHICAL POEMS

XXXII

The bulk of the poem develops ideas taken straight from the version of Aristotle's *Nicomathean Ethics* to be found in the widely read medieval encyclopaedia, the *Livres dou Trésor* of Brunetto Latini; March probably used the Catalan translation of this work. The philosophical theme here is that of the conditions for the practice of good. Surprisingly, at the end of the poem, March suddenly addresses a lady, 'Lily among thorns' to refer to his own sense of shame in relation to some aspect of his relationship with her, leaving the reader to ponder the overall meaning to be derived from the juxtaposition of two discourses of such different kinds.

LXXXII

An *esparsa,* or single-stanza poem (see also LXXX, LXXXI and LXXXIII) composed of examples from everyday experience of the unpredictable nature of Fortune (lines 1-3) followed by a series of sententious statements with strong Stoic overtones.

POEMS ON GRIEF

XCII

1-4 The 'hands' are those of Atropos, the Fate who cut the thread of life woven by her sister Lachesis and dealt out by a third sister, Clotho.

38 The still drop or *gutta serena* was a term used to describe amaurosis, a disease of the eye with no visible symptoms.

199-200 March here did not manage to leave the final couplet as a self-contained sentence, the only clear instance in the poem.

209-210 Here the translation ends in a rhyming couplet, much as March does in the other stanzas of the poems. I have not prioritized this aspect of the stanzas at all, and this is offered only as an example of the kind of concluding effect March meant his last two lines (which in several manuscripts are copied separately from the rest of the stanza) were meant to have.

245-246 In his final months March tried to arrange for the remains of his second wife, Joana Escorna, to be transferred to his own grave. The biographical connections could easily lapse into the macabre if taken too far, but March's documented attachment to his second wife (who bore him no children and thus did not found with March a dynasty for which a family vault would have had future significance) makes her a strong candidate for some or all of the six poems on grief.

XCIV

1 *sol en amor*: the phrase has the double sense of 'alone in love' (because of the lady's death) and 'unique in matters of love' (a claim March makes in many poems).

17-20 March alludes to the influence of the four humours on man in the course of the day; it was commonly believed that blood or choler was dominant from midnight until 6 in the morning, then bile until noon, melancholy from noon until 6 in the evening, and then phlegm until midnight; see C. S. Lewis, *The Discarded Image. An Introduction to Medieval & Renaissance Literature*, 1964; reprint Cambridge: Cambridge University Press, 1978, p. 173.

124 *veent-me lo món perdre*: literally, 'seeing that I lose the world'; here 'the world' means specifically the carnal pleasures of love, as the rest of the stanza makes clear.

A POEM ON GOD AND PREDESTINATION

CV

22 An iconographical reference to the outstretched arms of the crucified Christ.

29 The salvation of the good thief on Calvary (Luke 29.39-43) is used frequently in sermons of the time in relation to the doctrine of grace.

31 John 3.8: 'spiritus ubi vult spirat' in the Vulgate Bible ('the wind blows wherever it pleases' in modern English versions).

95 This idea derives from Job 10.4: 'Do you have eyes of flesh? Do you see as a mortal sees?'.

121-125 These ideas are developed above all in Galatians 3. 10-29 and 4.1-11.

199-200 In Matthew 26.24-25 Christ foretells Judas's treachery and alludes to his damnation. This is interpreted by some biblical commentators as clear evidence that Judas was a *praescitus*, a soul condemned from the beginning by the divine will.

201-203 Further allusions to the Book of Job: 'Why did I not perish at birth and die as I came from the womb?' (Job 3.11) and 'Why then did you bring me out of the womb? I wish I had died before any eye saw me. / If only I had never come into being, or had been carried straight from the womb to the grave' (Job 10.18-19).

213-216 March prays to receive the three theological virtues: faith, hope, and charity.

217-224 Attrition is a form of repentance without charity or love of God; contrition, true repentance, includes this theological virtue, and is the necessary condition for salvation.

FURTHER READING IN ENGLISH
AND MUSICAL VERSIONS

TRANSLATIONS

ARCHER, Robert, ed. & trans., 1992. *Ausiàs March. A Key Anthology* (Sheffield: The Anglo-Catalan Society).

CONEJERO, M. A., P. RIBES, & D. KEOWN, 1986-1989. *Ausiàs March. Selecció de poemes. Selected Poems* , 2 vols. (Valencia: Instituto Shakespeare Fundación).

TERRY, Arthur, 1976. *Ausiàs March. Selected Poems* (Edinburgh: Edinburgh University Press).

CRITICAL WORK

ARCHER, Robert, 1982. '"E ja en mi alterat és l'arbitre": Dramatic Representation in Ausiàs March's *Cant Espiritual*, *Bulletin of Hispanic Studies*, 59: 317-323.

–, 1983. 'The Workings of Allegory in Ausiàs March', *Modern Language Notes*, 98: 169-188.

–, 1985. *The Pervasive Image. The Role of Analogy in the Poetry of Ausiàs March*, Purdue University Monographs in Romance Languages, 17 (Amsterdam: John Benjamins).

–, 1988. 'The Conceitful Structure of Ausiàs March's Lo jorn ha por', *Revista Canadiense de Estudios Hispánicos*, 12: 191-206.

–, 1991. 'Tradition, Genre, Ethics and Politics in Ausiàs March's *maldit*', *Bulletin of Hispanic Studies*, 68: 371-382.

–, 1994. 'Ausiàs March as a Theorist of Love', in *A Discerning Eye. Studies Presented to Robert Pring-Mill on His Seventieth Birthday*, ed. Nigel Griffin *et al.* (Oxford: Dolphin), pp. 3-15.

BRENAN, Gerald, 1963 [1951]. *The Literature of the Spanish People* (Harmondsworth: Penguin), pp. 112-117.

CABRÉ, Lluís, 1996. 'Aristotle for the Layman: Sense Perception in the Poetry of Ausiàs March', *Journal of the Warburg & Courtauld Institutes*, 59: 48-60.

DI GIROLAMO, Costanzo, 1977. 'Ausiàs March and the Troubadour Poetic Code', in *Catalan Studies in Memory of Josephine de Boer*, ed.. Joseph Gulsoy & Josep Maria Solà-Solé (Barcelona: Hispam), pp. 223-237.

TERRY, Arthur, 1986. 'Introspection in Ausiàs March', in *Medieval and Renaissance Studies in Honour of Brian Tate*, ed. Ian Michael & Richard A. Cardwell (Oxford: Dolphin), pp. 167-177.

–, 1994. 'Ausiàs March and the Medieval Imagination', in *The Discerning*

Eye: Studies Presented to Robert Pring-Mill on His Seventieth Birthday, ed. Nigel Griffin *et al.* (Oxford: Dolphin).

–, 1998. '"Per la mort és uberta la carrera": A Reading of Ausiàs March, Poem 92', in *The Medieval Mind. Hispanic Studies in Honour of Alan Deyermond*, ed. Ian Macpherson & Ralph Penny (London: Tamesis), pp. 469-479.

–, 2003. *A Companion to Catalan Literature* (London: Tamesis).

WALTERS, D. Gareth, 1997. 'The Reader Misled and Empowered: Expectation, Ambiguity and Deception in Three Poems of Ausiàs March', *Bulletin of Hispanic Studies*, 74: 41-60.

–, 2002. 'Choosing March and Chosen by March: Imitation and Influence in Some Poems of the Spanish Golden Age', *Essays on Spanish Poetry of the Golden Age*, ed. Stephen Boyd & Jo Richardson (Manchester: University of Manchester Department of Spanish and Portuguese), pp. 163-177.

MUSICAL VERSIONS

The distinguished Valencian singer and songwriter Raimon has set to music seventeen of March's poems in the course of his career; these versions have done much to make March's work well known among the Catalan-speaking public. They are currently available in the following CDs, all of them accompanied by translations into English by Angela Buxton:

In *Per destruir aquell qui l'ha desert* (CD version Discmedi-Blau, DM 36602, 1988):
    'Així com cell [qui es veu prop de la mort]' (LXXXI)
    'Quins tan segurs consells [vas encercant]' (XI)
    'Veles e vents [han mos desigs complir]' (XLVI)
    'Sí com lo taur [se'n va fuit pel desert]' (XXIX).

Raimon. Integral (Auvidis A-6195, 1993), CD 6: 'Ausiàs March i alguns poetes dels segles XV i XVI' includes the above, and also:
    'Lo jorn ha por [de perdre sa claror]' (XXVIII)
    'No em pren així [com el petit vailet]' (LXVIII)
    'Si em demanau lo greu turment que pas' (LXXXVI)
    'No pot mostrar lo món menys pietat' (LXXVII)
    'No em fall record del temps tan delitós' (XXV)
    'On és lo lloc [on ma pensa repose?]' (LXXVI).

In *Cançons de mai* (Picap, 900100-03, 1997, CD):
  'Per servir amor' (= Tot llaurador [és pagat del jornal])' (LXXX)
  'Així com cell qui es parteix de sa terra' (CXI)
  'Sí co·l malalt [qui long temps ha que jau]' (LXXXIII)
  'Lo temps és tal [que tot animal brut]' (LXIV)
  'Quan plau a Déu [que la fusta peresca]' (LXXXII)
  'Així com cell qui en lo somni es delita' (I)
  'Alt e amor, [d'on gran desig s'engendra]' (III).

Raimon. Nova Integral Edició 2000 (Picap 90 0157, 2000. CD 10).
CD 7 (also available separately) contains all the poems set to music by Raimon.